THE CRITICAL ISSUES FACING
HIGHER EDUCATION
IN
HONG KONG

Ted Tat-Hong Poon

Table of contents

1   The Call of the Wild

- Paradigm shift initiated by changing part of a university from a government funded institution to a self-financed enterprise

Background

The University Grants Committee (UGC) of Hong Kong, the government funding agency of higher education, plans to reduce their funding to the higher education institutions of Hong Kong. Most of the institutions react to such a budget cut by changing part of their organizations to independent or semi-detached units that are going to run like profit making enterprises. This article[1] is going to examine the culture shift caused by such a change.

The scope of this article shall be restricted to things that happened before the beginning of academic year 2003-04. Occasionally, reports or materials that were published after August 2003 were cited in this article as examples to support the discussion but they would not be the main concern of this article.

---

[1] Part of this article, in a slightly modified form, was presented in the Conference on Internationalization of Lifelong Education: Policy and Issues organized by The Federation for Continuing Education in Tertiary Institutions, held in City University of Hong Kong, December 3-4, 2004. (Poon, 2004)

The higher education system of Hong Kong and its development

In 1989, the Hong Kong government estimated that a large number of highly educated Hong Kong citizens would leave Hong Kong before 1997. The capacity of the universities in Hong Kong should thus be increased drastically to compensate for such a loss. (Wu, 1998) Hence, the number of first-year-first-degree students of the University Grants Committee (UGC) funded programmes was thus increased drastically from about 7000 in 1989 to about 15000 in 1995. (See Appendix 1) Consequently, the government expenditure from higher education increased from 50 billion Hong Kong dollars in 91-92 to 100 billion Hong Kong dollars in 94-95 (Wu, 1998, p.183). Things kind of stabilized after 1995-96, and the number of first-year-first-degree students entering the UGC programmes stayed at the 14,000 level for the next few years.

In 2000, the government of Hong Kong announced another ambitious plan to enlarge the student body of the post secondary education. In his 2000 policy speech, the Chief Executive of Hong Kong set the target of letting 60% of Hong Kong senior secondary school leavers receive tertiary education within 10 years. (HKSAR, 2003) As a lot of the existing high school leavers could not meet the traditional entrance requirements of the regular degree programs, various supplementary programs like Associated Degrees or other sub-degree programs were expanded to accommodate this new influx of students.

Around 2001-02, the economic situation in Hong Kong started to deteriorate and the government planned budget cuts in all areas. The large budget of higher education caught the attention of a lot of people and there were discussion on whether the government funding was properly spent. It was under this situation that UGC announced the completion of Higher Education Review 2002 (hereafter HER). Lord Sutherland, chairman of the steering committee for HER and author of the report claimed: *"Changes are required to enable our institutions to be more flexible, out-reaching, innovative and focused in pursuit of their missions."* (UGC, 2002a, p.1) Change was basically what the Sutherland's report is all about.

The report was then accepted by the government after some minor amendments. (See Appendix 2) In the final version of the Sutherland's report, it was suggested that government funding would be awarded to the institutions in a more restricted manner. The higher education institutions were encouraged to seek their financial supports from both the public and the private sectors. More and more programs would be shifted from a government funded mode to a self-financing mode. The key point was: with the increase in emphasis on self-financing, these programs would be more profit oriented and would be operated just like commercial enterprises.

The Changes in the environment of the higher education industry

The discussion on the effects of the changes should first be started with an analysis to the macro environment of the higher education industry. Michael Porter's (1980) Five Forces framework will be used to analysis the environment of the industry

The first factor will be the Threat from new entrants. The entrance barrier to the higher education industry has always been very high. A higher education institution has to be licensed by the government under very strict conditions. Under the Sutherland's framework, establishing a new university in Hong Kong should become almost impossible. In addition, parents and employers are very sensitive to the name of the university one graduates form and brand loyalty can be considered as very high.

The second factor will be the bargaining power of the Suppliers to the industry. There are several major suppliers to this industry. As a supplier of land and public funding, the government always has a very high bargaining power. Charitable funds and other donors already had a very high bargaining power in the past. With the government's 'Matching fund' policy, the value of the private donations has actually been doubled and the influence of the private donation has thus been increased.

On the other hand, the teachers are suppliers of human resources and the overall bargaining power of teachers can be classified as decreasing. For the senior staff, most of them are tenured. Their reputation or qualification can help to attract students and research funding and they hence command relatively high bargaining power. For the more numerous junior teaching staff, their bargaining power are getting lower as the depressed economy prevents many fresh graduates from being absorbed by the commercial sector and they are forced to bid for an academic employment. Bargaining power for the non-academic staff also has decreased when the local unemployment rate increases. Bargaining power for other suppliers for equipments and facilities are usually not significant as there are many suppliers of such products.

Bargaining power of the customers, the third factors in Porter's framework, has become higher. If students can be considered as customers, their bargaining power has increased over the last few years as they had more programs to choose from. At the same time, in a depressed economy, fewer students can afford to go to university. The law of supply and demand dictates that for those lucky students who can afford to go to university, they will have higher bargaining power. Similarly, if employers are considered as buyers of the products of the universities, they will have high bargaining power as overall demand for university graduates has decreased and those employers who are still hiring can afford to be more demanding.

The fourth factor, the Threat of close substitutes has become higher. Close substitutes to local higher education shall be defined here as any other route through which Hong Kong students can get a degree or similar qualifications without leaving Hong Kong. Even though no new university can be established, more and more overseas educational programs can be offered locally. These programs are offered either directly through the distance learning mode of their operation or indirectly via partnership with local institutions. Being cheaper in price and more flexible in the entrance requirement, these overseas programs offer a very attractive alternative to the students - especially those students who have an intention to further their educations in overseas universities. It should be noted that overseas educational programs that require students to travel to overseas are usually much more expensive and are less attractive to the students, and thus their threat to the local institutions is relatively low.

Internal rivalry within the industry is the fifth factor. Given that the exit barrier for this industry is high and the marginal cost of serving additional clients is considered to be low, the existing players have a lot of incentives to stay and fight for the their survivals. The competition based on price and quality will become very intense and the internal rivalry of existing players shall increase.

All in all, strong competition among local higher education institutions is expected. This change in ecology of the higher education sector is bound to change the universities in Hong Kong.

How the universities would be changed

In his study on how organizational structure and behaviors are constrained and facilitated by forces in the environment of an organization, Carlson (1964) looked at how nature of the relationship between the organization and the clients will affect the organizational structure and behaviors of service organizations. Carlson divided service organizations into four different types according to their selectivity in client-organization relationship. Of special interest to this study are the Type I and Type IV organizations.

Type IV organizations are those cases where the clients and the organizations have no choice in establishing the client-organization relationship – public schools in US were cited as an example of this type of organization. Carlson described these service organizations as '*domesticated*'. In Carlson's (1964, p. 266) own words: "*By this simply meant that they are not compelled to attend to all of the ordinary and usual needs of an organization. By definition, for example, they do not compete with other organizations for clients; in fact, a steady flow of clients is assured. There is no struggle for survival for this type of organization. Like the domesticated animal, these organizations are fed and cared for. Existence is guaranteed. Though this type organization does compete in a restricted area for funds, funds are not closely tied to quality of performance. These organizations are domesticated in the sense that they are protected by the society they serve."*

On the other extreme, Carlson described the Type I organizations as the *'wild'* organizations. In this case, both the organizations and the clients have the power to decide whether they want to establish the client-organization relationship – private universities were cited as an example. Again in Carlson's own words (1964, p. 267): *"Type I organizations, on the other hand, can be called 'wild'; they do struggle for survival. Their existence is not guaranteed, and they do cease to exist. Support for them is closely tied to quality of performance, and a steady flow of clients is not assured. Wild organizations are not protected at vulnerable points as are domesticated organizations."*

By drawing on the similarity between organisms and organizations, Carlson wanted to make the propositions that, wild organizations, just like wild animals do behave differently from their domesticated counterparts. For example, the wild organizations tend to adapt to the demands of the environment much faster than the domesticated organizations.

In the era before suggestions listed in Sutherland's report became the government policy, the universities in Hong Kong

7

were similar to the '*domesticated*' organizations prorated under Carlson's framework. Being funded generously by the government, they had no fear of extinction. Clients and resources were guaranteed and there was no need for struggle for survival. [2] They adapted very slowly to changes in their environment. However, with the recent cut in funding, these organizations now need to fight for the resources and they have to struggle for survival. These organizations have become '*wild*' again. Consequently, it should be fair to expect that the structures, behaviors and the cultures of these universities are all going to change. It is the purpose of this study to investigate such changes.

Other reaction to these changes

Resource-dependence theory proposed by Pfeffer and Salancik (1978) suggests that when organizations face cut in their critical resource, they will react by trying to reduce their dependence on suppliers of that critical resource. They will adapt in way that can ensure the long term survival of their organizations. Hence, when faced with the threat of a cut in government funding, it is natural for the universities to look for ways to make them more independent from the government funding. Two of the common ways to reduce their dependences on the government are: seeking for private support through donation or technology transfer, and running profit-making educational and training programs.

---

[2] A generalized interpretation of Carlson's concept is adopted in here. It is not suggested that the universities have no right to select their students; rather the point that is emphasised here is that they are well supported by the government and they has no need to compete for survival.

Slaughter and Leslie (1997) studied how research universities, when faced with cutting in income, sought to create additional income by increasing their involvement in commercial operations. They called these *"institutional and professional market or market like efforts to secure external moneys **Academic Capitalism**"* (Slaughter and Leslie, 1997, p.8). In Hong Kong, most of the universities lack the resources or connections to benefit directly from commercial activities like that of a technology transfer. Hence, offering programs in a commercial mode seem to be the best way to secure additional money. This should explain why the size of the self financed segment of the higher education has grown very fast over the last few years. The places for the self-financed programs have grown from 6829 in 2001/02 to 12,275 in 2003/04. (Education & Manpower Bureau, 2003)

Segregation between funded units and self financed units

It should be noted that the universities try to segregate their funded units from their self financed units. One of the major reasons for this segregation is the pressure from the government. Universities like the Baptist University had been accused (UGC, 2003a and *Sing Tao*, 2003) of misusing of government fund by allowing the self-financed department to use the government funded services and facilities at improper transfer pricing. Other universities then tend to solve the problem by establishing units that are financially and operationally separated from the traditional units of the universities.

9

Another reason for this segregation is to protect the university proper from the students of the self-financed program. As most of the self financed programs have a lower entrance requirement than the traditional degree program, the students of these programs are perceived to be inferior to the regular university students. The management of the universities may want to keep these two groups separated to prevent any possible contamination. Some of the universities even have separated campuses for their self-financed units. Consequently, these self-financed units become financially, operationally and culturally segregated from their parents.

A case study: the story of the Department of Extramural Studies (DES)

The author worked in the government-funded department of a university until the end of 2002. When I was first transferred to the Department of Extramural Studies (DES) in early 2003, the 'culture shock' was really great. The ways people behaved in DES really remind me of the days during which I worked in the commercial world. Ever since the first day in DES, I keep comparing in my mind the environment of DES and that of my original department. I tried to reflect on why things happened like they did. The description and explanation I present below were the result of such a process which Ball (1996, p.167) described as a 'constant comparison'.[3]

---

[3] In Ball's own words: *"This sort of 'carry over' is an especially important part of the ethnographic process, I believe, ethnographers carry cases, slices of data, concepts around in their heads. Something like the procedures of 'constant*

Culture

According to Handy's (1993) Culture Types concept, well established traditional universities can be classified as the Person Culture. In this kind of culture, interaction among its members tends to be low and members are kind of worrying about their own business. In a traditional university, academics enjoy a very high degree of freedom in teaching and research. Control by management is usually considered as interference and is generally resisted by the academics (*Hong Kong Economic Times*, 2003). The subject of this study, DES, can be classified having a Power Culture, where the whole department is dominated by a very powerful leader (the head of the department) or a small group of people (the head plus his close associates). Decisions are made mostly by this so-called in-group and members outside of this inner circle have a relatively lower influence in the decision making process.

One component of the culture of an organization is the value or priority they assign to something. The best example on how the priorities of DES are different from that of the university is on the role of the students. Silver and Silver (1997) noted that neglecting students had been a venerable academic tradition and that tradition was still valid in the British university system. However, with the increase in the bargaining power of the students, this situation has to be changed. Talking about the increase in competition among British universities, Johnson and

comparison' goes on informally in work across cases, overtime, in different research projects." (Ball, 1996, p.167)

Deem (2003, p.292) claimed: *"The impact of greater competition between UK universities for students might be expected to result in more attention being paid to the needs of students by increasingly efficient and consumer-aware institutions and manager-academics."*

One of the direct impacts of this new status of the students is the increase in the influence of the students. Students play a more important role in the quality assurance and operation of the program. Some students see their roles change from a more passive stakeholder to a more aggressive power holder. (Ridgeway and Wallace, 1994) In DES's case, students had tried to influence the appointment of the lecturer by threatening that unless a specific person was appointed as their lecturer, they would leave the program and switch to a different school.

Another indirect influence of the student body is they increase the importance of the administration of the university. The student population of one of the DES programs had increased from 300 to 2300 in just two years. The drastic increase in student population explains the centrality of the administration. As explained by one of the interviewees in Johnson and Deem's study in British universities: *"If you have that rate of growth and you have enormous complexity of types of degrees, a lot of mature students, part-time students, students coming in for day release, afternoon release, evening, weekends ... the institution is running an inherently far more complex set of process than ever before. Sorry, but you can't do that without management ...* "(Johnson and Deem, 2003, p.298). The comment is also applicable to DES's case.

Leadership style

In the Patterns of school management for collaboration suggested by Caldwell and Spinks (1988), the ways through which leader make decision were classified into eight different levels. On one end of the scale is the most autocratic Level 1 that represents the case in which the leader makes all the decisions alone. At the other extreme is the most democratic Level 8 that represents the case in which everybody makes all the decisions together.

The leaders of a traditional university usually operate at the 7th level where the head and staff decide on a matter after seeking information and/or options from the community through a formal advisory structure. There are various committees and consultative channels which the leaders are expected to consult before reaching a final decision. The degree of collaboration is very high. Leader of DES usually operates at Level 4 in which the leader and his senior staff will make the decision after seeking information and/or opinion form the staff. The committees and other consultative mechanisms that are supposed to work as a check and balance are either so dominated by the leader that they cannot function properly or their opinions are simply ignored.

Borrowing from the idea of Blake and Mouton's Managerial Grid (1964), a two dimensional educational leadership grid is constructed. (See Figure 1) In this **Educator Grid**, educational leaders can be classified on a grid consists of two axes. The y-axis represents Concern for Business - regular business managers are expected to be high in this dimension. The other axis, the x-axis, stands for Concern for Profession – traditional

13

scholars and university academics are perceived to be high in this dimension. Yet the prefect leader for DES should be high, not just on the Concern for Profession dimension, but also reasonably high on the Concern for Business. Admittedly, this kind of leader is not easy to find.

Figure 1: Educator Grid

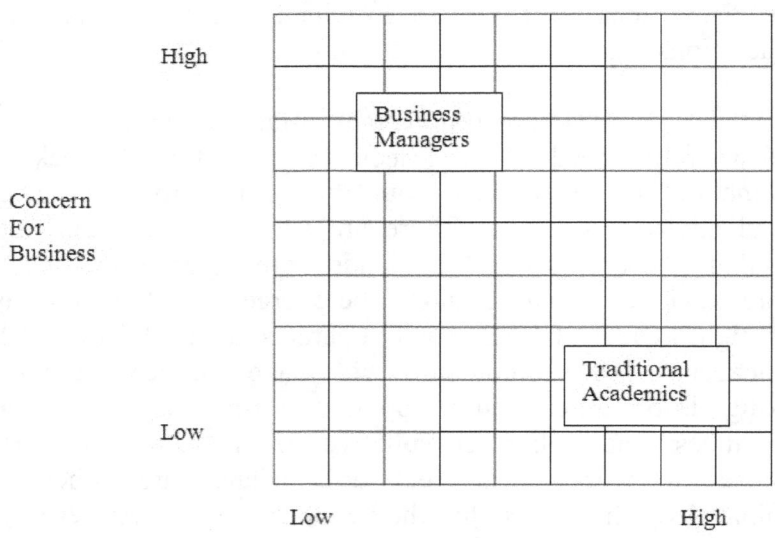

Concern For Profession

Management Practices

The Management of DES try to create the impression that they are really concerned about the quality of teaching by setting up various control and monitoring mechanisms that are supposed to guarantee the quality of teaching and learning. Yet most of these mechanisms also tend to create a lot of additional work to the already overloaded staff. In the words of Johnson and Deem, *"Manager-academics at all levels described the phenomenon of 'proceduralisation' as vast increase in bureaucratic, administrative and paper-based work resulting from external and internal quality assurance"* (Johnson and Deem, 2003, p.303).

At the same time, strict behavioral controls are applied to the academics both within and outside classrooms. For example, when they are not teaching, academic staff are told to stay in their office from nine to five just like factory workers. Whenever they had to leave their seats for any extended period of time, they are expected to place a note in their doors stating clearly where they have gone. The management also tries to control what the academics can do inside the classroom. For example, teachers of pre-packaged program were instructed not to ask students to give presentations in the class when students complained to the department head that it was a waste of the students' time. In other words, instead of controlled by culture or educational objectives, academics in DES have to face very strict behavioral control. To certain extend, DES is run more like a factory than a university.

Strategy

Being a self financed operation, it is very important that DES can meet the demand of its target customers. Unlike the traditional academic department, DES is not constrained by the human resource it has when they decide what subject they can/should offer. The major objective is to get the first mover advantage – which is defined as meeting the demand before anyone else can. As such, the prime objective is to find out what/where will the demand be and then produce a product to satisfy such a demand.

According to Miles and Snow's (1978) concept, a traditional university can be classified as an 'Analyzer' that moves into new markets and products only after extensive evaluation and market research. On the other hand, DES can be classified as a 'Prospector' that activity seek out new markets for their products and then jump right into any opportunity that emerge on the horizon.

The turn-around time for DES to come up with a new program can be very short. The syllabus of a new subject can be generated within a couple of days by a staff who may have very little idea of what the subject is all about. Getting a teacher to teach the subject is just one of the minor details much like getting a vacant classroom for the class. Both processes properly will not have to be worried about until the subject has been offered and enough students have signed up for the subject.

The high responsiveness of DES can be an advantage as it can respond very fast to any opportunity that presents itself in the market. Yet the same high responsiveness often causes erratic changes in its strategic planning.

Structure

Instead of the traditional functional departments system used in many of the university, the structure of DES can be better described as a matrix in which the academics are grouped, according to their backgrounds, loosely under several subject areas like business, marketing or information technology. The academics are then assigned to work in different programs as a program leader. In theory, each of these programs is also supported by a program officer and a few program clerks. The whole structure is best described as a matrix system in which the academics are now project leaders supported by a few functional staff.

The picture would be quite different if the power structure was analyzed. In a traditional university, the academics are located on the top of the power pyramid and they have close connections with the administrators, the students and the part-time teachers. In DES, the situations are quite different. Administrators have the dominate position and they dominate the connections with the Part-time teachers and even the students. The reason for this change would be explained in the Power Shift section. (See Figure 2)

Figure 2: Comparison of Academic lead structure and Administrator lead structure

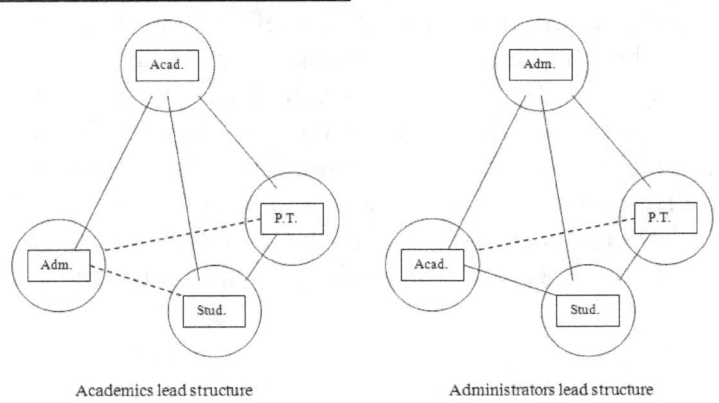

Academics lead structure   Administrators lead structure

17

--------- Loose connection _____ Close connection

Acad: Academics
Adm.: Administrators
Stud.: Students
P.T.: Part-time teachers

Human resource management

In terms of Human Resource philosophy, the cost conscious DES management tends to consider the staff more like a resource similar to a machine or equipment in a factory. The best way to utilize this resource is to lower the costs (by hiring fewer workers with lower salaries) but maximizing the benefits (by increasing their workload or assigning more duties to them). This is quite different from the more traditional approach in which the staff is considered as a source of great potential. If they can be placed in the right condition to release their great potential by teaching with innovative approaches or more inspiring sprits, they can make greater contribution to the organization.

With the increase in emphasize of cost-effectiveness, contract employment become more popular than tenure. It has been reported (*Sing Pao*, 2003a) that universities tried to cut cost by many ingenious approaches. One of these approaches involves cutting all the non-teaching responsibilities (like research or administrative duties) off the teacher but also cut their salary by half. Another approach is to treat the teachers like factory workers and paid them only according to the hours that they teach.

18

These cost conscious approaches can quickly change the culture and balance of power in the universities. Being marginalized and segregated from the administration of the university, these 'teaching machines' have no significant influence in the key decision process of the department. As they are usually hired on rather short term contract, the decision of renewal (or non renewal) of their employment contracts can actually exert a constant pressure in these academics. The management can thus place a much tighter control in the academics who would have much less bargaining power to resist such controls.

The recruitment of temporary staff can also lead to a problem. Just like what has been discussed in the Strategy section, DES offer courses in any field that the Administrators think has a market potential. The market demand for these courses can be very unpredictable and the administrators usually have to wait until the very last minutes before they decide on whether the course will be offered. Consequently, DES often needs to recruit a large number of temporary lecturers within a rather short period. Unfortunately, this recruiting-as-needed system reduces the chance for DES to recruit the best staff. What is interesting in this case is that in an industry that depends so much on the quality of services/products, there is so little emphasis on the quality assurance of the staff who directly delivers these services.

Occasionally, part time teaching staff are recruited based on the recommendations from people of importance. These candidates may be highly qualified but they lack the experience or commitment to do a good job in teaching. The management is usually very reluctant to replace these temporary lecturers for fear that someone may lose *'face'*. The existence of such 'untouchables' causes a lot of problems for other academic staff members on the same team.

In recruiting, staff members with multiple skills are preferred over specialists. The reason behind this practice is rather simple: due to the unpredictability of course offering, DES needs a pool of staff that can take up any teaching assignment with a very short notice. Thus multi-skilled staff with a diversified background or training can offer this flexibility much easier than specialists.

Last but not the least; the staff are sometime selected not necessarily on their qualification or experience, but more on how much it costs to hire them. There have been reported (*Ming Pao*, 2003) that some staff with higher qualification were not hired even when they applied for teaching posts in DES. The reason was simply that their salaries were too high.

Power shift

With the establishment of self financed departments that emphasizes more on efficiency than on anything else, the role of the administration has become more important. There were also reports on universities continuously recruiting non-teaching staff in face of funding cut and such a practice often led to overstaff in administrative side of the universities. (*Sing Pao*, 2003b) In some universities, full time academic staff only account for less than 40% of the total staff. (Shi, 2003)

Talking about the relationship between the academics and managers of universities, Johnson and Deem claimed (2003, p.306) "*Deans and HoDs who deal with academic staff on a direct basis need on-going experience in teaching and research, in order to sustain understanding of, and credibility with, their colleagues."*

In the case of DES, most of the administrators never have any actual teaching experience or teacher training. At the same time, the only management experiences they can claim are what they had accumulated during their employments in DES. It is not surprising that when the administrators proclaimed that it was of pedagogical importance for the staff to follow some procedures or policies, a lot of academics found these statements to be not very convincing.

As stability of tenure of the teaching staff is not considered to be important, the turn over rate of the academics (under both part time and full time employments) has been relatively high. The continuity of a subject or even a program was then hinged on the hands of the administrators who usually have a much lower turn over rate. According to the model constructed by French and Raven (1959), the administrators possessed a lot of power.

The administrators possess the expert power since they control the information related to the course and its operation. As the administrators are usually designated as the contact point with the internal and outside parties, the administrators can easily dominate the communication channels and cut the information off the academics. In the words of Pfeffer (1996, p.111) *"... power is a function of one's position in the network of communications and social relations, where this position is assessed not only simply in terms of structural centrality, but also in terms of the power of the people with whom one is connected."*

21

The administrators also control the reward and coercive power since they have great influence on recruiting and or renewing the contract of the part time teachers. There were many occasions in which part-time teachers were hired by the administrators without even consulting the opinion of the academics who were responsible for the quality of teaching in that programs. As far as the part-time teachers were concerned, the administrators were really the only people they should have to please.

Really, the only source of power that the academics can rely on is their legitimate power. Whenever there are academic staff, who is presumably the leader of the program, do not see thing the same way as the administrators, the administrators can easily out maneuver the academic staff by going above their heads and seek the sympathetic ears of the more senior management. With their long term relationship with the top management of DES, they tend to have a much better chance to obtain the support of the senior management who will then overrule the decision of the academics.

Similar conclusion can be drawn if the Authority-Influence framework presented by Bacharach and Lawler (1980) is applied. Here the academics hold the formal aspect of power. They are formally sanctioned by the organization to make the final decisions. They also hold the authority to demand submission from their supporting administrative staff. However, the administrators are those who hold influence. They have no formal right to make decision but they can exert a lot of power due to their personalities, expertise, or opportunity. In a fast changing environment like the one faced by DES, power structure tends to be rather ambiguous and administrators who rely on influence can actually control the running of the program.

An example: The teaching of the pre-packaged programs

Being a self-financed unit, DES likes to offer any program that is marketable. However, properly due to fear of 'unhealthy' competition, DES is not encouraged to offer their own version of some popular programs that are currently offered by other departments in the university proper. DES by-passes these restrictions by forming a partnership with overseas universities and than offer the overseas partner's pre-packaged programs in Hong Kong. The courses of these programs are usually designed by the foreign universities which control the aim, objectives, tasks, course materials, timetables, assignments and examinations. In theory, local teachers of these courses can teach these courses very efficiently as they are required to follow the prescribed course materials and no additional preparatory works in curriculum and teaching approach are required.

At the same time, students for these overseas programs are usually assessed by standardized examinations prepared by the overseas institutions. The students demand the teachers to follow the course materials very closely as they fear that if the teachers do not cover everything in the syllabus, they will not be able to answer some questions in the standardized examination. This belief actually takes away any chance for the teachers to use any creative or innovative teaching approaches as they tend to be considered as 'irrelevant' and 'a waste of time'.

The comment of Kydd (1997) regarding the impact of pre-packaged course on teachers can be used in here to describe the situation: *"For teachers this means that where once they were able exercise considerable professional autonomy over the selection of knowledge and the ways it would be taught, their activities in the classroom are now more tightly controlled. This leaves teachers with less room for exercising both professional autonomy and professional authority"* (Kydd, 1997, p.115).

Unfortunately, as all the teachers are required to follow the materials like a robot, the professional knowledge required for teaching these pre-packaged course are perceived to be very low. Hence the administrators develop the impression that 'anybody' can teach these courses. Academics teaching these courses enjoy a rather low social status as they are doing a job that 'anybody' can do. They have now become a 'Jack of all trades' but can claim to be 'master' of none.

Conclusion

Management of universities must be very careful in how they handle the environmental changes if they want to maintain the treasured heritages of their organizations. Suggestions to the management on how to prevent some of these undesirable effects of the changes include:

- Reasonable targets should be established. Staff should not be pressured to accept targets that are too ambitious or they may do things that may not fit the best long term interest of the institution. For example, setting target that push to double the enrollment of a program in one year may push the staff to accept unqualified applicants just to meet the quota.

- Simultaneously loose and tight control should be applied. In their discussion on excellent organizations, Peters and Waterman (1982) proposed that excellent performance can be achieved if the organization adopted simultaneously loose and tight organization. It is suggested in here that the staff of DES should be indoctrinated with belief in educational excellence via proper socialization, share of values and effective communication. On the other hand, the organization should be loosely organized with less rigid rules and regulation that give rooms for professional autonomy and creativity. After all, *"The best teaching builds upon the creative talents of lecturer and professor"*. (Sutherland, 2002, p.44)

- Leader of these self-financed units should be selected carefully. A suitable leader for this kind of business like self-financed unit need proper balance between concerned for profit and education. Using the concept of Educator Grid that was proposed in previous section, a good leader for DES should be balanced in his business and profession orientation. Traditional academics tend to be too insensitive to profit and costs and hence may not be too suitable for a self financed unit. Yet the business manager type may be too concerned for profit and may ignore the importance of protecting the valued culture of the university.

- Job rotation (or other forms of exchange of personnel) should be used to ensure a homogenous culture among various units of the university. One way to increase the homogeneousness of the university is to rotate staff among the more academic oriented departments of the university proper to the more profit oriented institution like DES so they can learn from each other. Another approach to achieving similar result is to use more staff from the university proper as part time or visiting lecturers in DES. The culture of the university can then be diffused to DES. However, for this kind of socialization to work, the staff involved should be seasoned enough so they are well vested with the traditions of the university.

It should be pointed out that the Sutherland's report actually predicted some of these changes in the landscape of the post-secondary sector. As Sutherland claimed: *"Together, these proposals amount to a dimensional, paradigm change for Hong Kong's education system, rather than minor change. It will shift Hong Kong's higher education system from an elite system, focus exclusively on academic attainment and aimed at the top 20%, to a mass education system. Accompanying this will be a shift in the culture of higher education from closing gates (to control supply) to building bridges (to drive and meet demand)"* (UGC, 2003, p.52). Whether these changes are really that beneficial to the Hong Kong higher education system remain to be seen.

Acknowledgement

The author would like to thank Professor Eric Hoyle of University of Bristol for his suggestions and comments on the draft of this article.

Bibliography

1. Bacharach, S. and Lawler, E. (1980), *Power and Politics in Organizations*, San Francisco: Jossey-Bass.
2. Ball, S. (1996), "Power, conflict, micropolitics and all that!" in Walford, G. (Ed.) *Doing Educational Research*, London: Routledge.
3. Blake, R. and Mouton, J. (1964) *The Managerial Grid*, Houston: Gulf
4. Carlson, R. O. (1964) "Environments, constraints and organizational consequences", in Gridffiths, D. et. al. (eds.) *Behavioural Science and Educational Administration*, Chicago: U. Chicago Press.
5. Cladwell, B. and Spinks, J. (1988) *The Self-Managing School*, London: Falmer.
6. Education & Manpower Bureau, (2003) *"LEGCO QUESTION NO.6 : Post-secondary education in Hong Kong"* Available at: http://www.postsec.edu.hk/eng/lcq6030709.asp. Accessed: 2 December 2003.
7. French, J. and Raven, B. (1959), "The Bases of Social Power" in Cartwright, D. (ed.) *Studies in Social Power*, Ann Arbor: University of Michigan Press
8. Handy, C. (1993) *Understanding Organisations*, 4th ed., London: Penguin
9. Hong Kong Special Administrative Region (2000), Chief Executive's Policy address 2000, Available at: http://www.policyaddress.gov.hk/pa00/eindex.htm, (accessed: 20 December 2003)
10. *Hong Kong Economic Times*, (2003) "Management of the HKU is backward, expert suggested simplification of organizational structure" (in Chinese), 8 February.

11. Johnson, R. and Deem, R. (2003), "Talking of students: Tensions and contributions for the manager-academic and the university in contemporary higher education", *Higher Education,* 46: p.289-314

12. Kydd, L. (1997) "Teacher professionalism and Managerialism", in Kydd L, Crawford, M and Riches, C. (eds.) *Professional development for educational management,* Buckingham: Open University Press.

13. Lau, C. K. (1998), "A lesson in management", *South China Morning Post,* Aug 4.

14. Miles, R and Snow, C (1978) *Organisational Strategy, Structure and Process.* New York: McGraw-Hill.

15. *Ming Pao,* (2003) "Teachers with high qualification were not considered due to their high salaries" (in Chinese), July 07, p. A17.

16. Peters, T. and Waterman, R (1982) *In search of excellence: lessons form America's best-run companies,* Cambridge: Harper & Row.

17. Pfeffer, J. & Salancik, G. (1978) *The external control of organizations: A resource dependence perspective.* New York: Harper & Row

18. Pfeffer, J. (1996) *Managing with power – Politics and influence in organizations,* Boston: Harvard Business School Press.

19. Poon, T. (2004) "Who would become a successful leader of the School of Continuing Education: academic, educator or administrator?" *Conference of Internationalization of Lifelong Education: Policy and issues.* City University of Hong Kong, December 3-4. The Federation for Continuing Education in Tertiary Institutions, Hong Kong.

20. Porter, M. (1980) Competitive strategy: *Techniques for Analysing Industries and competitors.* New York: Free Press.

21. Ridgeway, C and Wallace, B. (1994) *Empowering Change. The role of people management.* London: Institute of Personnel and Development
22. Shi, L. (2003), "From the pay of the university president to the structure of the university", (in Chinese), *Hong Kong Economic Times*, May 22, pp.P24.
23. Silver, H and Silver, P. (1997), *Students: Changing roles, changing lives.* Buckingham: Open University Press.
24. *Sing Pao*. (2003a) "Baptist University push for part time teacher" (in Chinese), September 10, p.A12.
25. *Sing Pao*, (2003b) "Universities show mismatch of resources, 4000 more administrators than teachers" (in Chinese), Dec-09, p. A10
26. *Sing Tao*, (2003) "Universities are suspected of subsidizing self-financing program" (in Chinese), Nov 19, p.F01
27. Slaughter, S. & Leslie, L. (1997) *Academic capitalism – Politics, policies, and the entrepreneurial university.* Baltimore: The Jones-Hopkins University Press.
28. Sutherland, S. (2002), *"Higher Education in Hong Kong - Report of the University Grants Committee commissioned by the Secretary for Education and Manpower"*, Available at: http://www.ugc.edu.hk/english/documents/UGCpubs/her_e.html. Aaccessed: 10 December 2003.
29. University Grants Committee, (2002a), *Higher Education Review,* Available at: http://www.ugc.edu.hk/english/documents/press/her2603e.html., Accessed: 22 December 2003.
30. University Grants Committee, (2002b), *UGC's Final Recommendations,* Available at: http://www.ugc.edu.hk/english/documents/press/pr271102e.html. Accessed: 10 December 2003.

31. University Grants Committee, (2003a) 2nd TLQPR of Hong Kong Baptist University (Sept 2003). Available at: http://www.hkbu.edu.hk/2nd_tlqpr/. Accessed: 18 December 2003.

32. University Grants Committee, (2003b) UGC statistics, student numbers. Available at: http://www.ugc.edu.hk/english/statistics/Chart.pdf. Accessed: 18 December 2003.

33. Wu, S. (1998), *Hong Kong education from the point of view of an educator*, (in Chinese) Hong Kong: Guang Jue Jing.

2 Changes in the Hong Kong higher educational system since 1997

Introduction

Many authors (for example, Law, 1997; Mok and Lee, 2000; Chau and Chan, 2001; Ku, 2002; Luk, 2002; Postiglione, 2002; Post, 2003) have discussed changes to the higher educational (HE) system in Hong Kong. The objective of this article[1] is to analyse examples of recent changes in the HE system of Hong Kong and demonstrate how they are related to changes in the political and economical environment since 1997.

Instead of using the general Social-Technological-Economical-Population-Legal (STEPL) model commonly used in strategic management textbooks like Thompson and Strickland (2001) to analyse the macro business environment; the framework proposed by Thomas and Postlethwaite (T&P) in 1983 will be used to examine the factors that influence the rate and completeness of such changes.

The framework developed by T&P is chosen partly because it is a model designed for the analysis of educational changes in Asia. The other advantage of using this model is that Thomas (1983: 265) had applied this model to analyse the educational system in

---

[1] Part of this article, in a slightly modified form, was presented in the Conference on Internationalization of Lifelong Education: Policy and Issues organized by The Federation for Continuing Education in Tertiary Institutions, held in City University of Hong Kong, December 3-4, 2004. (Poon and Lee, 2004)

Hong Kong in 1983 and Bray (1999) had also used this model to analyse the Hong Kong educational system shortly after 1997. Together, these researchers have provided a very useful platform for an analysis of Hong Kong's higher educational system in 2004.

The Thomas and Postlethwaite framework

In T&P's model (1983: 7), a *force* or *cause of change* is defined as *"a factor whose presence is necessary for an event to occur. Without each of the forces that press against each other in a kind of dialectical exchange, the event could not have happen the way it did"*. Thomas and Postlethwaite (1983: 10) further classified the positive forces that hasten changes as (1) *Enabling* forces which are the causal conditions that provide an opportunity for educational innovation but are not directly involved in the change, and (2) *Direct-positive* forces which are the forces that apply specifically to that process of change. As the reciprocal of the above forces, they also classified the negative forces that retard change as *Disabling* and *Direct-negative* forces.

It should be pointed out that any significant change in the educational system is seldom the result of any single cause. T&P (1983: 7) also emphasize the fact that they believe in the principle of m*ultiple causation*. That is *"… an event is not simply the result of a single force but is always the result of many forces, some of which may be more powerful than others and therefore more worthy of note in an analysis of the causes or an event"*.

32

This principle of multiple causation also applies to both *"the horizontal and vertical dimension of the timing of an event"*. Horizontal dimension of timing is defined as *"several forces converge simultaneously to mould an event"*. And vertical timing is defined by a sequence of events that accumulate over time to bring about the change. So, *"... behind each cause is an earlier cause which brought the later one about"* (T&P, 1983: 8). Obviously, it is not practical to trace back the origin of the causes to too far back in the history thus this essay will only focus on the events that happened after 1997.

In their framework, Thomas and Postlethwaite (1983) further classify the significant forces into seven dimensions: Magnitude of intended change; availability of alternatives; motivation or philosophical commitment; social and organisational stability; resource accessibility; organisational and technical efficiency; and adequacy of funding. (See Appendix 1). Bray (1999: 236) combines the last three dimensions into one single dimension – resources. Judging from the complexity of the economical/financial activities of modern educational systems (Slaughter and Leslie, 1997), Bray's approach may be a more practical approach and hence will be adopted in this essay.

Comparison of T&P framework against STEPL model

Upon closer examination of the T&P framework, it should not be difficult to note that there are many overlaps between the Enabling forces of the T&P framework and the elements of a traditional macro environmental analysis model (e.g. STEPL: Social-Technological-Economical-Population-Legal) used in business strategic analysis. A comparison of these two models is presented in Appendix 2.

The major differences between the T&P framework and the STEPL models are in two aspects. Firstly, the T&P framework is more specific in nature. For example, instead of the general technological level of the country/city, T&P framework focuses on *"advanced communication and transportation facilities"* which are factors directly related to the spreading of ideas and distribution of educational materials. Secondary, the T&P framework specifies the direction and magnitude of the forces that is required to enable or disable the changes. For example, a small population and a small territory are considered as enabling forces that favour changes, where as a large population and a large territory are considered as disabling forces that prevent changes from happening. In the following sections this directional aspect of the T&P framework will be de-emphasised as it can be demonstrated that some of the disabling forces can also be the factor that hasten change[2].

Hong Kong as a city for change

Under the T&P's framework, Hong Kong is under the influence of many enabling forces which together can make Hong Kong a city that is very susceptible to change. It has a rather small territory with land area of only 1103 square kilometres and its communication and transportation facilities are very advanced.

---

[2] Even though continuity of the ruling government is considered as an enabling force that hastens changes, it is obvious that the change of ruling government can also create a need and the environment necessary for educational change. (e.g. Post, 2003)

These two factors alone ensure that new ideas and materials can spread through the city easily. With the bilingual training for a large proportion of the population, the society has long been exposed to international ideas as well (Bray, 1999: 231). The same degree of internationalisation can be observed in its tertiary institutions. Scholars of many different origins have been teaching in the universities in Hong Kong for many years. Data reported by Postiglione (quoted in Bray, 1999: 232) indicates that a significant proportion of the academic staff in the higher educational institutions is either of foreign origins or has been trained in overseas universities. Hong Kong has long been considered as an open society with a high proportion of people holding international views.

As for peace and amity in the society, Hong Kong has been relatively stable in the political sense during the several decades after the Second World War. Hence there has not been much significant disruption in educational system in Hong Kong. However, as the date when Hong Kong will be returned to China, approached, Thomas (1983: 270) observed "*a sense of impermanence*" that was cast over Hong Kong. Observations of this kind were also echoed by Cheng (1995: 1) who described the uncertainties felt not just by him but also by many people just before 1997. For obvious reasons, it was undesirable to create more anxiety in people's mind during the final few years of the British rule. Hence stability was a goal pursued by both the British and the Chinese governments and thus the finals years of British rule were characterised by very cautious changes (Bray, 1999: 235). Now that the 1997 issues had become part of the history, the Hong Kong government has been much more aggressive in implementing educational changes.

Changes in social system, however, can take many different forms. Luk (1992: 117-118 as quoted by Bray 1999:235) discussed the significant of the process of industrialization that changed Hong Kong from 1950 onwards. He suggested that these processed had *"... profoundly changed the occupational profile, appropriate knowledge, necessary skill, and general attitudes"* of the Hong Kong society. Perhaps the same things can also be said about the de-industrialization of Hong Kong and the resulting financial depression that had hit the people of Hong Kong around 1997. Hong Kong now has almost no industry and businesses that were prosperous during the last decades have to look for different ways to survive under this transformation of economy. This tends to create the need for changes in the objectives as well as the format of HE.

The original T&P framework (1983) classified resources related forces into three dimensions: Resources accessibility; organisational and technical efficiency; and adequacy of funding. In more modern terms, resource accessibility is related to the hardware of the society. It deals with the facilities, equipment and technologies used in education. Organisational and technical efficiency refer to the software of the society and it covers how different components of the educational system are fitted together. The last item, adequacy of funding refers to the amount of total financial resources that are available in the society and how much of such funding is allocated to the education innovation.

As far as education hardware is concerned, Hong Kong has been rather advanced in areas like Internet and computer technology (ICT). ICT based education is becoming more popular due to the wide spread usage of computers at home and at work. ICT affects education in many different aspects. Different teaching approaches like web based teaching, on-line assessment and pooling with hand held computers have become popular in universities. ICT also makes new program for continuous education possible. Both foreign universities and local universities in Hong Kong have introduced various cyber or virtual universities (for example, Hong Kong CyberU) and offered university level programs to students located in many different places.

As for funding, Hong Kong government has been quite generous in financing higher education. The per student recurrent spending for the Hong Kong HE (in constant 2000 HK$) has been increased from HK$134,869 in 1991/92 to HK$166,114 in 2000/01 (Post, 2003). T&P (1983:35) pointed out clearly that sufficient funding is required to bring about changes, but what they had not specify is that reduction in funding can be a even bigger force to bring about drastic changes. The direct impact of funding in the HE system of Hong Kong will be discussed in later sections.

According to the T&P framework, the only force that tends to retard changes in Hong Kong is its large population. With a population of 6.8 million in 2003 (Hong Kong Census & statistic Department, 2004), Hong Kong has a larger population than over 50 sovereign states in the world. (Bray, 1999) One thing that is rather unusual is that this population of Hong Kong is rather homogeneous in ethnic background and more than 98 percentage of the population are Chinese who write and read the same language - Chinese. Even though the original framework of T&P (1983) tends to suggest that large population is a disabling force for change, Hong Kong should be considered as an exceptional case as its compact and homogenous population, together with highly efficient system of communication overcome most of the barriers created by a large, and hence generally diversified, population.

All in all, it can be concluded that there are many enabling forces supporting changes in the Hong Kong higher educational system. The HE system of Hong Kong is a dynamic system that is very accessible to changes. In the following section, examples of changes in the HE system will be discussed with reference to the direct forces that have direct impact in the HE system.

Forces that apply specifically to changes in HE system of Hong Kong

T&P (1982:14) treated educational change as a rather positive thing and they linked educational changes to catch phrases like *"innovation"*, *"modernization"* and *"new"*. Positive factors like *"Amicable relations among the education-system's staff members"*; *"efficient, nearby sources"* which was the distribution of equipment and personnel; and *"advanced organizational structure"* were required for educational changes to take places. Hence, all of the above mentioned factors are classified as "direct-positive forces" that hasten changes and the opposites or reciprocals of these factors will be the direct-negative forces that retard changes.

This viewpoint is quite acceptable if educational change is taken as building a new university or establishing a new training institution. Yet if educational change is interpreted in a more neutral sense as an "alternation[3]" or "transformation" of the

---

[3] Based on the *Longman Dictionary of the English Language* (1984), p242.

existing educational system, then it can be argued that even direct-negative force like lack of resources can also lead to educational changes. The situation is like rolling a ball on the ground. The motion of the ball is determining by the topography of the ground (the enabling forces), and the direction and strength of the force that acts directly on the ball. The conceptual diagram of this modification is presented in Appendix 3.

In the following sections, three educational changes in the HE system of Hong Kong will be analysed and the direct-positive and direct-negative forces that hasten these changes will be identified.

1. Expansion of the HE system

T&P (1983: 31) predicted that social instability could serve to initiate innovation. 1977 was such a big change in the social environment of Hong Kong it bounds to lead to many changes. As early as 1989, the Hong Kong government estimated that a large number of highly educated Hong Kong citizens would leave Hong Kong before the change in ruling government in 1997. The capacity of the universities in Hong Kong was thus increased drastically by the Governor David Wilson partly to compensate for such a *"Brain-drain"* and partly as a *"gesture to restore public confidence"* (Post, 2003).

However, Asian financial crisis, mistakes in government policies, restructuring of the economy, and the increase in competition due to the growth of other near-by cities have caused a depressed economy in Hong Kong (Lui, 2002). As

T&P projected, change in resources can be a direct positive force for educational changes. The post 1997 government were thus looking for ways to save money and there were discussion on whether the government funding was properly spent in HE. In November 1999, the secretary of education and manpower, Joseph Wong Wing-ping indicated that the post-secondary education had *already* grown enormously and the participation rate of university had reached 18%. The government had no immediate plans for further expansion (Post, 2003)

Yet, in his 2000 policy speech, Mr. Tung Chee Hwa, the Chief Executive of Hong Kong, set the target of letting 60% of Hong Kong senior secondary school leavers receive post-secondary education within 10 years (HKSAR, 2000). Even though Tung's announcement can be interpreted as merely a restatement of his previous decisions to expand education for technical and economically instrumental reasons (Post, 2003), a lot of people interpret his statement as a promise to increase the student population of HE. As the traditional degree programs could not meet the demand of this sharp increase in student population and the government did not promise an increase in funding to expand the traditional university programs, new self-financed supplementary programs were needed to accommodate this new influx of students.

The *"leaders"* of the continuing education divisions of the Hong Kong universities are *"committed"* to this idea as they embrace this as a chance to *"help these once-peripheral divisions lead themselves forward and market their services to the public"* (Post, 2003: 992) . As T&P suggested, for a society like Hong Kong that interacts freely with other societies, changes come relatively easy when the leaders welcome changes. *"More educational innovation occurs when the schooling establishment is directed by leaders who seek new ideas, welcome the importation of new options, and stimulated members of the school system to create alternatives themselves*" (T&P, 1983:23).

'Alternatives' like Associated Degrees and other supplementary programs were quickly created and the number of Hong Kong higher educational institutions offering post-secondary programmes has increased drastically in recent years. For example, during the short period between academic year 2001/02 and 2003/04, the number of institutions offering full-time accredited self-financing post-secondary programmes had increased drastically from 11 to 20 (Hong Kong Education and Manpower Bureau, 2004). At the same time, the number of post-secondary programmes offered by these institutions had increased from 41 to 123.

'New options' are also "*imported*" from overseas and there has also been a great increase in the number of foreign institutions that offer courses or programs that lead to formal academic qualifications in Hong Kong. Through the schemes of non-local courses provided under the *Non-local Higher and Professional Education (Regulation) Ordinance*, overseas institutions offer post-secondary level courses either independently or through collaborations with local organizations. In 2001, there were a total of 645 courses offered under this scheme (Hong Kong Education and Manpower Bureau as quoted in Evans and Tregenza, 2002:43). By early 2004, this number had jumped to 909 (Hong Kong Education and Manpower Bureau, 2004a).

2. The re-linking with the Chinese Higher Educational System

For many years, the higher educational system of Hong Kong has long been de-linked from its counterparts in the mainland. For political reason, the colonial government had taken a very subtle approach in manipulating the curriculum to de-emphasis people's emotional association with Hong Kong and China. Luk (2003:28) argued that "... *generations of Hong Kong Chinese pupils grew up, learning from the Chinese culture subjects to identify themselves as Chinese but relating that Chineseness to neither contemporary China nor the local Hong Kong landscape*".

This system of isolation generally works quite well in the primary and secondary level. Its effectiveness in post-secondary level, however, had not been prefect. Law (1997) described how universities students in Hong Kong had developed a strong emotional attachment for the mainland in the 70's under the "knowing the home country" movement. This China heat, however, cooled down during the 80's and 90's after more realities of the political situation like the Cultural Revolution became known in Hong Kong. After the Tiananmen Square incident in 1989, some of the university academics and students had developed a more critical stance toward the Chinese government. This sentiment had become part of the resistance force against the 'Recolonization' of the HE system of Hong Kong by the Chinese government (Law, 1997).

As 1997 approached, the government recognized that this kind of emotional detachment should be changed. As proclaimed by the government, "*At a time of political transition, we need our citizens to actively adopt a new national identity, and to be participative and contributive to bring about smooth transitions, to sustain prosperity and stability and to further improve the Hong Kong society"* (Education Department, 1996:21 as quoted in Bray, 1997:16). On the *"educational leader"* side, the Secretary for Education and Manpower, Arthur Li, had openly expressed his regrets that the Hong Kong students could not have a better understanding of the home country as they were educated under the colonial system (*Hong Kong Commercial Daily*, 2004/April/20). With the support of the government, many people had strong motivation to re-nationalize the Hong Kong people. According to T&P (1983), how successful this re-linking process can be will be dependent on the balance of forces between the leaders (e.g. government officials) who are strongly committed to this change and the educational leaders (e.g. some academics in HE) who choose to resist such a change.

In the HE system, this re-linking with the mainland higher educational system takes many different forms. The most common form of this re-linking will be the introduction of more "Chinese elements" into the curriculum. The case study presented by Chau and Chan (2001) demonstrated how this is usually accomplished. In light of the "1997" issue, the Department of Accountancy of their university *"has initiated major changes in its accounting curriculum..."* and *"the revised accounting curriculum has undergone major changes in response to the needs generated by the reunification and the accounting reforms in China"* (2001:153). Emphasis is now placed on different subjects and different skills *"... to cope with the dynamic business environment in the 21st century and the needs of the Chinese accounting discipline"*. In other words, the linkage is easily established by realigning the emphasis on knowledge and skills according to what is required in the environment of the mainland.

Another way to realign the Hong Kong HE system with that of the mainland is to change the format of the whole program. The proposed Three-to-Four scheme is for changing the British based three years university system to the four years system used in the mainland. Some educators like the president of the Chinese University emphasised the educational benefits of this change in increasing the chance for a more holistic education (*Sing Tao Daily*, 2004 July 02). Other educators like the chairman of the Union of higher education academic staff are more open in describing this scheme as a way to remove the barrier that block the flow of students from the mainland to Hong Kong (*Wen Wei Po*, 2004 April 14).

Actually, the re-linking of the HE system through the recruitment of students across the border has started in a limited scale for some years. Starting in 2004, the Hong Kong government announced that the quota of non-local students in the universities would be doubled (Ng, 2004b). At the same time, the Chinese authorities had also announced that the universities in Hong Kong could now start recruiting self-financed students directly from mainland with much less restriction than before (*Oriental Daily*, 2004a). The universities in Hong Kong welcome this new arrangement as they see these self-financed students as a new source of income that can generate the much needed revenue for the universities (*Hong Kong Economic Times*, 2004b).

On the other hand, leaders of the universities from mainland are probably more concerned about non-economic factors. Hong

Kong students who are accepted by the mainland universities will get sponsorships that cover all their expenses plus a job offer when they graduate. One of the conditions is, however, that the students must support the One-country-two-systems principle and the Basic Laws (*Hong Kong Economic Times*, 2004c).

The re-linking can also be achieved by ensuring that proper personnel can be utilized to influence the HE system of the other side. As T&P (1983: 15) suggested *"The use of efficient, nearby sources for producing the equipment and personnel required in the intended educational change"* is one of the positive forces that can hasten changes. In his discussion of the *"Recolonisation"* of the Hong Kong HE system, Law (1997: 199) described how, starting in early 1990, *"the Hong Kong government began to incorporate PRC academics into its higher education to represent the PRC's interests"*. These *'recolonisation agents"* can facilitate the re-linking process in both the policy making level as well as the operational level of the HE system.

T&P (1983:16) also suggested that *"advanced organizational structure"* or proper mechanism should be established so changes can be easily channelled to the needed places. With the recent introduction of the Mutual Recognition of Academic Degrees in Higher Education (Hong Kong Education and Manpower Bureau, 2004b), designated bodies can now have the official channel to *"provide professional advice to higher education institutions in both places on the comparability of systems and academic degrees in higher education in both places with the aim of facilitating academic exchange and co-*

operation". To what extend will this *"advice"* affect the HE system of Hong Kong remains to be seen.

3. Funding and government control of the universities

Talking about people's motivation to change, T&P (1983:24) remarked that people who are to carry out the change *"… must feel sufficient fear of not changing, or else they must be enticed by the prospect of sufficient reward for participating in the change"*. Hence, powerful leaders that *"have sanctions or propaganda techniques"* can influence educational personnel to support whatever change demanded by the leaders.

Sanctions are exactly how the Hong Kong government can influence the higher educational institutions. As early as 2000, the government, through the University Grants Committee (UGC) had started a mechanism of withholding 2% of the government grant to the universities. This money will be given to the universities only when they are willing to modify their programs according to the instruction of the government (*Hong Kong Economic Times*, 2004a). In the few years that followed, this approach has been so effective that its use has been expanded.

By the academic year 2005, UGC will withhold 10% of the annual funding allocated to each institution (Ng, 2004a). This money will be given to the institutions only if they comply with their roles assigned by the government. (See for example, The Hong Kong Polytechnic University, 2004b). Institutions that perform excellently according to the instructions may even be rewarded with additional funding. The Committee Chairman Alice Lam was quite open in explaining that the funding

46

mechanism would effectively prevent institution from going out of their roles. She was quoted "*It is a deterrent. The institutions will be penalised if they do not performed well*". It should not be a surprise that the universities have to dance to the magic tone of the government.

Conclusion

The general environment and some specific examples of the educational changes in the Hong Kong HE system were analysed according to the key points identified by the T&P framework. As an analytical framework, the T&P framework is found to be useful in identifying the key elements that should be addressed in an analysis. However, its power in predicting the consequence caused by any specific factor is insufficient to cover all the situations.

By applying the enabling force concept of the Thomas and Postlethwaite framework, the HE system in Hong Kong is found to be very dynamic as most of the environmental factors tend to favor changes. The direct force aspect of the T&P model were used in identifying the key elements present in three of the major changes namely: the expansion of the HE system in Hong Kong; the re-linking of the HE system in Hong Kong and the mainland; and funding and government control of the universities. It can be concluded that the causes of these changes are related to not only economical factors but political ones as well.

Acknowledgement

The authors would like to thank Dr. Leon Tikly of the University of Bristol for his suggestion and comments on part of the draft.

Bibliography

Apple Daily (2004) "Last year population was 6.81 million; just increase 0.35%, lowest increase since returning to China" (in Chinese). February 18, p.A12.

Bray M. (1997) "Education and Colonial Transition: the Hong Kong experience in comparative perspective". In Bray M. and Lee W. (eds.) *Education and Political transition: implications of Hong Kong's change of sovereignty.* Hong Kong: Comparative Education Research Centre.

Chau G. and Chan T. (2001) "Challenges faced by accountancy education during and beyond the years of transition – some Hong Kong evidence". *Journal of Accounting Education.* 19:3, Autumn, pp.145-162.

Chan, M. (2002) "Introduction: The Hong Kong SAR in Flux". In Chan, M and So A. (eds.), *Crisis and Transformation in China's Hong Kong.* Armonk: Sharp.

Cheng, J. (1995) *Hong Kong education during political transformation.* (In Chinese) Hong Kong: Oxford University Press.

Cummings. T. and Worley, C. (2001) *Organisational Development and Change*, 6th ed. Cincinnati: South-Western.

Evans, T. and Tregenza, K. (2002) "Asian students' experience of studying overseas courses". In Murphy, D.; Shin, N. and Zhang, W. (Eds.) *Advancing Online Learning in Asia.* Hong Kong: Open University of Hong Kong Press.

Hang Seng Bank Limited (2004) Employment challenges. *Hang Seng Economic Monthly*. March.

Hong Kong Census & Statistic Department (2004) Population and Vital Events. Available at http://www.info.gov.hk/censtatd/eng/hkstat/hkinf/population_index.html. Accessed 2004/May/17.

Hong Kong Commercial Daily (2004) "Arthur Li: It is natural for Hong Kong people to be pro-China" (in Chinese). April 20, p.A05.

Hong Kong Education and Manpower Bureau (2004a) "Statistical Information". Available at http://www.emb.gov.hk/index.aspx?nodeID=75&langno=1. Accessed 2004/April/18.

Hong Kong Education and Manpower Bureau (2004b) "Memorandum of Understanding between the Mainland and Hong Kong on Mutual Recognition of Academic Degrees in Higher Education". Available at http://www.emb.gov.hk/index.aspx?nodeID=2491&langno=2. Accessed 2004/April/18.

Hong Kong Economic Times (2004a) "Five universities perform well in division of labour – total bonus of 25 million dollars was rewarded" (in Chinese). March 25. pp.A34.

Hong Kong Economic Times (2004b) "City University struggles to attract students form the mainland, hoping to increase to 150 students" (in Chinese) April 21. pp.A23.

Hong Kong Economic Times (2004c) "Beijing and Qing Hua University accept students without examination" (in Chinese). June 07. p.A22.

Hong Kong iMail (2002) "Academics join in call for Arthur Li apology". October 24.

Hong Kong Polytechnic University (2004a) "New Human resource model approved". *Staff newsletter of The Hong Kong Polytechnic University*. March/April 2004. Available at http://www2.polyu.edu.hk/script/staff/ePost@PolyU. Accessed 2004/March 04.

Hong Kong Polytechnic University (2004b) "Role of PolyU re-affirmed". *Staff newsletter of The Hong Kong Polytechnic University*. March/April 2004. Available at http://www2.polyu.edu.hk/script/staff/ePost@PolyU. Accessed 2004/March 04.

Hong Kong Special Administrative Region (2000), "Chief Executive's Policy address 2000", Available at: http://www.policyaddress.gov.hk/pa00/p66e.htm. Accessed: 17 July, 2004.

Jegede, O. (2001) "Hong Kong". In Jegede, O. and Shive, G. (eds.) *Open and distance education in the Asia Pacific Region*, p.44. Hong Kong: Open University of Hong Kong Press.

Ku, A. (2002) "Postcolonial cultural Trends in Hong Kong: Imaging the Local, the National, and the Global". In Chan, M.

and So, A. (Eds.), *Crisis and Transformation in China's Hong Kong*. Armonk: Sharp

Law, W. (1997) "The accommodation and resistance to the decolonisation, neocolonisation and recolonisation of higher education in Hong Kong". *Comparative Education*. 33:2. pp.187-209.

Lei, J. (2003) "This is not the way to manage university education". (In Chinese). *Ming Pao*. November 19. p.D8.

Lui, F. (2002) "Hong Kong's Economy since 1997". In Chan, M and So A. (eds.), *Crisis and Transformation in China's Hong Kong*. Armonk: Sharp

Luk, B. (2003) "Chinese culture in the Hong Kong curriculum: heritage and colonialism". In Stimpson, P.; Morris, P.; Fung, Y. and Carr, R. (Eds.), *Curriculum, Learning and Assessment: the Hong Kong experience*. Hong Kong: Open University of Hong Kong Press.

Mok, K (1999) "The cost of managerialism: The implications for the 'McDonaldisation' " of higher education in Hong Kong. *Journal of Higher Education Policy and Management*. 21:1, pp.117-127.

Mok, K and Lee, H (2000) "Globalization or re-colonization: higher education reforms in Hong Kong". *Higher Education Policy*. 13, pp.361-377.

Ming Pao, (2003) "City U Associate program plans for 35% salary reduction, increase teacher to student ratio and new staff will be hired only under contract system" (in Chinese). October 03. p.A16.

Ming Pao, (2004) "Polytechnic University resumes renewing long term employment contracts with staff" (in Chinese), April 14, p.A02.

Ni, Q. (2004) "American educational exhibition attracts thousands" (in Chinese). *Apple Daily*. April 4. p. A10.

Ng, T. (2004a) "Universities set performance targets". *The Hong Kong Standard*. January 31. p.B06.

Ng, T. (2004b) "Colleges to target overseas students". *The Hong Kong Standard*. April 21. p.B03.

Oriental Daily (2004a) "Hong Kong universities will be able to recruit students from the mainland" (in Chinese). April 8. p. A24.

Oriental Daily (2004b) "Low birth rate causes 22 kindergartens to close down" (in Chinese). April 8. pp.A24

Poon, C. (2003) Script delivered in RTHK radio programme "Letter to Hong Kong" on 1 November 2003.

Poon, T. and Lee, C (2004) "Globalizing or re-linking: establishing a closer relationship between the higher education system in Hong Kong and the mainland". Conference of Internationalization of Lifelong Education: Policy and issues. City University of Hong Kong, December 3-4. The Federation for Continuing Education in Tertiary Institutions, Hong Kong.

Post, D. (2003) "Post-secondary education in Hong Kong – Repercussion for inequality and civil society". *Asian Survey.* 43:6. pp. 989-1011.

Postiglione, G. (2002) "The transformation of Academic Autonomy in Hong Kong". In Chan, M and So A. (eds.), *Crisis and Transformation in China's Hong Kong*. Armonk: Sharp.

Shive, G. (1992) "Educational Expansion and the Labor Force", in Postiglione, G. and Leung, J. (eds.) *Education and society in Hong Kong: Toward one country and two systems*. pp. 215-231. Hong Kong: Hong Kong University Press.

Slaughter, S. and Leslie, L. (1997) *Academic capitalism – Politics, policies, and the entrepreneurial university*. Baltimore: The Jones-Hopkins University Press.

So, A and Chan, M. (2002) "Conclusion: Crisis and transformation in the Hong Kong SAR – Toward Soft authoritarian Developmentalism?" In Chan, M and So A. (Eds.) *Crisis and Transformation in China's Hong Kong*. Armonk: Sharp.

Sutherland, S. (2002), '*Higher Education in Hong Kong - Report of the University Grants Committee commissioned by the Secretary for Education and Manpower*', Available at: http://www.ugc.edu.hk/english/documents/UGCpubs/her_e.html. Accessed: 10 December 2003.

Thomas, R. (1983) "The two colonies – A prologue". In Thomas, R. and Postlethwaite N. (eds.) *Schooling in East Asia – Forces of change*. Oxford: Pergamon Press.

Thomas, R. and Postlethwaite N. (1983) "Describing change and estimating its causes". In Thomas, R. and Postlethwaite N. (eds.) *Schooling in East Asia – Forces of change*. Oxford: Pergamon Press.

Thompson, A. and Strickland, A. (2001) *Crafting and Executing Strategy – Text and Readings*. Boston: McGraw Hill.

University Grants Committee, (2002a), *Higher Education Review,* Available at: http://www.ugc.edu.hk/english/documents/press/her2603e.html. Accessed: 22 December 2003.

University Grants Committee, (2002b), *UGC's Final Recommendations,* Available at: http://www.ugc.edu.hk/english/documents/press/pr271102e.html. Accessed: 10 December 2003.

University Grants Committee, (2003a) 2nd TLQPR of Hong Kong Baptist University (Sept 2003). Available at: http://www.hkbu.edu.hk/2nd_tlqpr/. Accessed: 18 December 2003.

Zheng, C. (2003). "The causes of funding cut of the universities" (in Chinese). *Hong Kong Economic Journal*, November, 19, p.9.

Appendix 1: The Thomas & Postlethwaite Classification of Determinants of Change and Non-Change

Positive Forces that Hasten Change	Negative Forces that retard change
Dimension 1: Magnitude of Intended Change	
1. 1 Population Size and Accessibility	
Enabling forces: small population. Small territory, easily traversed terrain and waterways, mild climate. Advanced communication and transportation facilities - radio, telephone, television, electronic-computer systems, fast trains, ships, autos, aeroplanes	*Disabling forces:* Large population. Large territory, rugged terrain and treacherous water ways, severe climate. Primitive communication and transportation facilities
1.2 Complexity of Intended Change	
Direct-positive forces: A few simple aspects of the education system to be changed.	*Direct-negative forces:* Many interrelated aspects of the education system to be changed.
Dimension 2: Availability of Alternatives	
Enabling forces: A society with a high proportion of people holding modernisation views. A society that interacts freely with other societies and encourages new ideas.	*Disabling forces:* A society with a high proportion of people holding traditionalist views. A society isolated from interaction with other societies and that discourages innovation
Direct-positive forces:	*Direct-negative forces:*

Educational leaders who seek new ideas and encourage varied opinions and proposals.	Educational leaders who defend traditional practices, discourage differences of opinion and new proposals.

Dimension 3: Motivation or Philosophical Commitment	
Enabling forces: A society with a high proportion of people holding modernisation views.	*Disabling forces:* A society with a high proportion of people holding conservative, traditionalist views.
Direct-positive forces: A high proportion of powerful educational leaders strongly committed to effecting the proposed change. Leaders have sanctions or propaganda techniques available for influencing educational personnel to support the change.	*Direct-negative forces:* A high proportion of powerful educational leaders who lack a strong commitment to the change or, more seriously, who choose to resist the change. Leaders have sanctions or propaganda techniques available to influence educational personnel to resist the change.

Dimension 4: Social and Organisational Stability	
Enabling forces: Peace and amity in the society, continuity of the ruling government, regular production of sufficient goods to meet people's needs.	*Disabling forces:* War, revolution, rioting, frequent changes of government, and such 'natural' disasters as floods, earthquakes, and crop failures.
Direct-positive forces: Amicable relations among the education-system's staff	*Direct-negative forces:* Dissension among the education-system's staff

members, rewards to staff for efficient service, clear leadership direction, infrequent organisational change.	members, jealousies, frequent organisational change, frequent displacement of existing projects with new projects, lack of rewards for efficient service.
Dimension 5: Resource Accessibility	
Enabling forces: A society with advanced industries and training systems.	*Disabling forces:* A society whose services for producing supplies and training personnel are few and inefficient.
Direct-positive forces: The use of efficient, nearby sources for producing the equipment and personnel required in the intended educational change.	*Direct-negative forces:* The lack of efficient, nearby facilities for producing the equipment and personnel required for the educational change.
Dimension 6: Organisational and Technical Efficiency	
Enabling forces: A society with efficient organisational structures and a high degree of specialisation, technical expertise and advanced equipment for producing objects, processing data, communicating, training people, and the like.	*Disabling forces:* A society with ineffective organisational structures, little technical expertise in performing specialised tasks, and little or no advanced equipment for producing objects, processing data, communicating, training people and the like.
Direct-positive forces: The application in the educational	*Direct-negative forces:* An educational change system

change system of advanced organisational structure, efficient specialisation, a high level of skill in the specialised tasks, and advanced equipment to perform tasks that are more effectively done by machines than by people. An effective method for adapting these systems to the local culture.	that is inefficiently organised or poorly suited to the local culture, that involves little or no specialisation or expertise in performing specialised tasks, and that uses no equipment for performing tasks - that is, the system uses only people.

Dimension 7: Adequacy of Funding	
Enabling forces: A society with enough wealth to expend large sums for improving services, including educational services.	*Disabling forces:* A society marked by widespread poverty.
Direct-positive forces: Educational change advocates who present a convincing case for their projects are receiving a high priority in obtaining available education funds.	*Direct-negative forces:* Other agencies or projects that make a more convincing case for deserving funds to support their projects than is made by advocates of the change-project under review.

Appendix 2: Comparison between T&P's enabling forces and the STEPL framework

Dimension in T&P Framework	T&P's enabling forces	Corresponding elements of STEPL framework
1	"Small population"	Social
	"advanced communication and transportation facilities"	Technology
2 and 3	"A society with a high proportion of people holding modernisation views. A society that interacts freely with other societies and encourages new ideas."	Social
4	"Peace and amity in the society, continuity of the ruling government"	Political
	"regular production of sufficient goods to meet people's needs"	Economical
5	"A society with advanced industries and training systems"	Technology
6	"A society with efficient organisational structures and a high degree of specialisation,"	Social
	"technical expertise and advanced equipment for producing objects, processing	Technology

	data, communicating, training people, and the like."	
7	"A society with enough wealth to expend large sums for improving services, including educational services"	Economic

Appendix 3: Conceptual diagram of the modified Thomas and Postlethwaite framework

Direct forces: factors that have direct impact on the system and determine the direction and the extent of the change

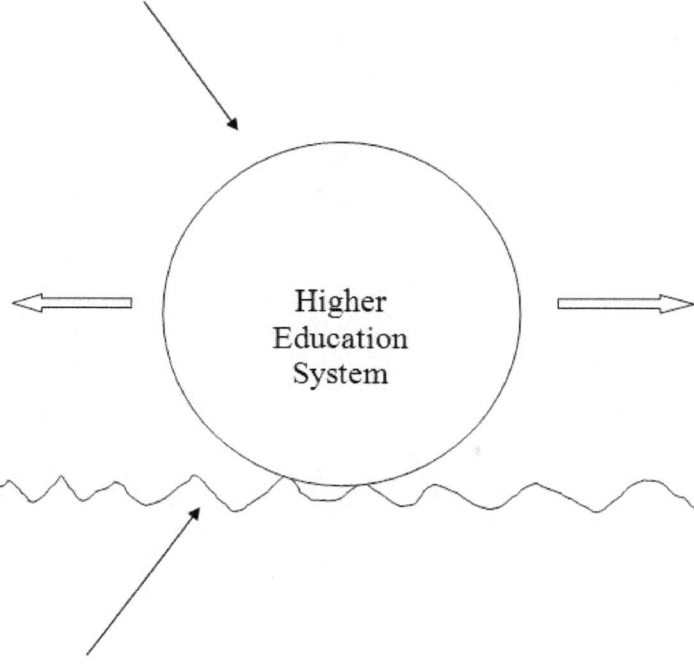

Enabling/disabling forces: factors that determine how dynamic the system can be

3   Students' view of professional behaviours of part-time lecturers in higher education[1]

Introduction

Part-time lectures (PTL) have been the topics of many studies. (Gappa & Lesile 1993; Jacobs 1998; Fenwick 2003; Sophos 2003; Thorsteinson 2003; Toutkoushian & Bellas 2003). In their study of PT faculty in US higher education, Gappa & Lesile (1993: 18) find: "Part-timer are exceptionally well qualified for their assignments and part-timers are a rich resource to higher education, with much to offer to their students and their institutions". In a more recent study of PTL in US community colleges, Lesile & Gappa (2003) suggest that long-term returns in teaching effectiveness and morale can result if colleges can invest in the PTL's capacities and not treat them just like replaceable parts.

Universities in Hong Kong have employed PTL for various purposes. PTL are used frequently to supplement regular fulltime faculty in universities that have high fluctuation in their enrolments (*Ta Kung Pao*, 2004/May/08). Universities also use part-time employment to access some lecturers who, because of their other obligations, would not be hired as a fulltime lecturer (*Hong Kong Economic Times* 2003/May/15). Special talents are sometimes recruited under a part-time basis to teach some

---

[1] Part of this article, in a slightly modified form, was presented virtually at the International Conference of Education, Research and Innovation 2008, The International Association for Technology, Education and Development (IATED), Madrid, Spain, 17-19 November. (Poon, 2008)

special subjects or share their special experiences (*Hong Kong Economic Times* 2004/Apr/23).

In recent years, many Hong Kong education organisations are hiring more and more PTL. One of the major reasons for this trend is the increasing need to save money (*Sing Pao*, 2003/Sep/10). PTL are paid only for the hour they teach and thus money for employee benefits and other personnel expenditure is saved. A common application of this concept is to rehire downsized or retired lectures on a part-time basis and pay them a reduced salary. A modification of the above approach is simply paying existing lecturers half of their previous salaries but the lecturers will focus just on teaching and will not be involved in administrative duties or research.

Teachers as professionals

Different researchers discuss the concept of a professional teacher from many different aspects of this profession (Hoyle & John, 1995). The professionality of teachers is analysed from different perspectives – professional status, professional behaviours, professional identity, professional autonomy, professional knowledge, professional authority, and professional responsibility.

Kydd (1997) explains that people try to prove the professional status of teachers by comparing teaching against other traditional professions such as law, medicine and careers in the church. Some common criteria are then identified which can then be used to gauge the degree to which a group can call themselves a profession and enjoy the privileges enjoyed by such a profession. In Kydd's words (1997:111)

> *Thus claims to professional status have derived from the exercise of professional judgement, professional autonomy, the right to self-regulations, expertise in a body of knowledge highly valued by society and a relationship with the 'client' based on common understandings of 'mutual' good* (Humes, 1986).

In the current study, the discussion will be focused on teachers' professional behaviours since the behaviours of teachers have very direct impact on what is happening in the classrooms. In Hargreaves's words (1994:10): "Despite all the investment in staff development and in-service training, classroom teaching, even for teachers, remains central to the definition of what teaching is".

Bloomer (1980) tries to justify that teachers are professionals via first distinguishing a professional by how the person discharges his duties and "an attitude of mind". In Bloomer's words (1980:362)

> *A professional is employed to carry out his work with a high degree of competence and with reasonable diligence. This will tend to necessitate a flexible approach to working hours and job definitions. A professional is called upon to exercise responsible personal judgement based on specialized knowledge. He is independent of immediate supervision and detailed control; he*

has full charge over the discharge of his immediate area of professional responsibility.

He then argues that teachers are professionals as they exhibit certain behaviours which are generally the characteristics of a profession.

Most teachers are deeply involved in their work. They think and talk about it whenever a group of them are gathered together. A substantial, arguably excessive, degree of responsibility is accepted for the development of their pupils. Work extends far beyond school hours and school terms; indeed for many teachers the boundary between work and leisure is often ill-defined.

The difficulty of this approach is that it requires that the behaviours of teachers are reasonably standardized and can be proven to fit the requirements before it can be claim that the whole group are professionals. These standardized behaviours can then be called professional behaviours as they help to establish teachers as a profession.

However, these standardized behaviours may be defined quite differently under different conditions. Some practices that are considered "expected" behaviour under one environment may not be counted as part of the professional requirements under a different environment. In their comparison between French and English teachers, Broadfoot & Osborn (1993) argue that teachers often have some expectation toward themselves and there are some professional responsibilities that teachers always consider their jobs. *"Defining what is to be learned"*, *"Accepting responsibility for social and personal outcomes of schooling"*, and *"Evaluation of pupils"* are considered as the basic tasks that teachers are expected to handle. However, Broadfoot & Osborn go on and pointed out that there are differences in the professional responsibilities perceived by French and English teachers and hence there are differences in the content and scope of what the teachers generally accepted as their standardized behaviours.

As such, when the professional behaviours of teachers are being discussed, it must be clearly stated that the discussion is based on the 'restricted' professional role (Hoyle, 1974) which focus more on the teachers' immediate responsibility and classroom concerns, or the 'extended' professional role which extended to the teachers' engagement with issues, structures and practices beyond their own classrooms.

In Hong Kong, various parties have publicized their visions of the professional behaviours of the teachers. For example, The Council on Professional Conduct in Education (1995) published a *Code for the Education Profession of Hong Kong* that prescribes how teaching profession should interact with the profession, students, colleagues, employer, and parent/guardians. The code, in its discussion for the "Commitment to students" specifies how professional educators should behave in the classroom. However, this code treats the issue more like a "legal" requirement than a "guideline for good teaching practices".

Universities in Hong Kong often issue their own in-house version of code of practices. The *Code of Ethics for Teaching* issued by the Hong Kong Polytechnic University (2004) gives five general principles to guide the teachers' behaviours and conducts. Even though the five general principles of the code: *commitment to quality education; fairness; respect; integrity; and confidentiality* are also illustrated by examples, they are still too abstracted for day-to-day usages. For a more specific guideline on teaching behaviour, a teacher has to refer to the document titled "*Some suggestions on the Criteria for Basic, good and outstanding Level of Teaching*" (The Hong Kong Polytechnic University 2004)[2]. In this document, (see Appendix 1), Basic, Good and Outstanding behaviour standards of teacher are listed out and can be used by the university to rate its teaching staff.

Why PTL are not considered a professional

Upon closer examination of the above documents, it can be found that for a lecturer to be rated as "Good" or even "Outstanding", he or she has to perform well in a lot of areas and at very different levels. Some requirements that can be easily met by full time faculty can be quite difficult or even impossible for PTL. For example, all lecturers should "Communicate clearly with students" and "Marks work diligently and fairly, and gives useful feedback to students". However, as most of the PTL have other obligations during their non-teaching hours; it is much more difficult for PTL to "Be available, and approachable, for consultations by students". Similarly, PTL often are hired to teach pre-packaged course developed either by other full time faculty of the same university; or by faculty of some overseas universities that

---

[2] Similar documents can probably be found in other Hong Kong universities like the Open University of Hong Kong (1999).

license their programs to the Hong Kong universities. In either case, the common examinations which are generally used in these kinds of classes also put a lot of pressure on the teachers to teach the standardized curriculum according to the prescribed ways. There is really not much room for the PTL to manoeuvre and be creative. Hence, not too many PTL can "Produces useful teaching resources and handout materials for students" and actually use them in their classes.

By the same token, it is difficult for a PTL to perform well in "Involvement in subject/programme development and administration" and "Anticipates and takes a proactive role in meeting changing conditions so as to maintain and enhance the quality of teaching and learning". In fact, most of the PTL do not have much chance to communicate with students or their colleagues outside the classroom hours. Also, PTL can say very little about how their working environment should be managed as they seldom participate actively in the administration of the institution. In the author's experience of teaching as PTL for more than 10 years, there were only a few occasions during which PTL are encouraged to take an active role in really changing something. Hence it is not surprising that PTL are sometimes degenerated into what Goodson & Hargreaves (2003:127) describe as "technical deliverer of guidelines and schemes derived elsewhere".

In short, most of the criteria (for example, research, course development, program development) that are used to measure teacher's behaviours in universities are geared more toward the full time faculty and cannot reflect the ways PTL operate. Hence, PTL are usually not honoured as good performers according to the traditional criteria of good teaching. It should be mentioned that some universities set up a modified guidelines to guide the behaviours of the PTL (see for example, The University of Hong Kong, 2003). However, the guidelines tend to be more like "Help Tips" for teaching and cannot be used to gauge the behaviours of the PTL in their working context.

It is important to point out that the author is not saying that there is no PTL who demonstrate really professional behaviours in their jobs. Over the years, the author has met and heard of many PTL who have shown high dedication and enthusiasm in their teaching. Occasionally PTL are honoured by their universities (see, for example, The University of Hong Kong, 2001). It is just that they are not earning the credit that they deserve because the measuring system is tilted more toward activities outside the classrooms.

Yet classroom teaching and its related activities are things that are rated very important from the viewpoints of the students (Rego, 2003). The views of the students are important as the students are the stakeholders who are most directly affected by the behaviours of the PTL and their opinions more reflect the attitude of the public. As Hargreaves suggests (1994:14)

> *When members of the public judge teachers, and do so on the basis of the many teachers they themselves have known over the years, they judge them through children's eyes – eyes that have seen the teacher teaching, but not preparing, making or meeting.*

As the higher educations have shifted more and more toward self-finance mode, it is logical to evaluate the behaviours of the

PTL from the point of view of its most important stakeholder – its students. This study will identify professional behaviours of the PTL that are valued by their students and hence should be emphasised by the university and the teachers.

Methodology

In this pilot study, quantitative data were collected by survey. The survey was designed according to the approach suggested by Cohen and Manion (1994). Questionnaire was used because it is very effective in collecting information from a relative large group of students.

Students were asked to identify the traits and behaviours of a good PTL that they had encountered over their years of study. The survey asked students to think of the good PTL when they ranked, in a Likert scale, how close the statements in a 32 items list matched the traits or behaviours of the good PTL. A sample of the questionnaire is listed in Appendix 2. The answers were then compared against data obtained by other researchers.

The list of the traits and behaviours was constructed based on the samples of traits and good behaviours identified by students in a pilot study in which the students were asked to describe the traits and the behaviours of a very good PTL that they had encountered during their years of study. The criteria they used to describe their candidates were compiled into a list. The idea of this design is to determine if the students perception of a good lecturer are influenced by the traits like social and academic status of the PTL. In the traditional hierarchy of a university, PTL usually do not enjoy a very high organizational status.

Separating the traits and the practices can reduce the halo effect of perception.

Convenience sampling was used in this study. Different groups of students who had attended the classes taught by the author were contacted by e-mail and invited to fill out the attached questionnaire. The background of the students were different in gender (male/female), subjects of study (Strategy, Human Resource Management, Change Management), year of study (from less than 2 years to more than 6 years since they completed their Secondary Five), and level of study (Graduate, Undergraduate and Sub-degree). About 90% of these students are part time adult students. Only about 10% of the students are younger students from the full time programs.

In order to overcome possible bias, all the data in this investigation were collected via anonymous questionnaires. The questionnaire was sent to a list of about 115 valid e-mail addresses of students. Students can choose to either reply by e-mail or, if they prefer, return the completed questionnaire by fax which then would not reveal the identity of the sender. To avoid any conflict of interest, students were assured repeatedly that their grades would not be affected by the nature of comments they made in the questionnaire. Students were also told clearly that the author is not a PTL and hence should be ignored when they fill out the questionnaire.

Data presentation and analysis

Altogether 33 replies were received and the return rate was 28.7%. The returned questionnaires were also checked for integrity and samples that showed indication of obvious

72

unreliability would be discarded. One of the questionnaires was discarded because of incompleteness and the other 32 replies were used.

Data from all the completed questionnaires were then entered into the SPSS program. Descriptive data were first drawn from the general population to identify items that reflect the attributes or behaviours of a good PTL. Data were also analysed by the Pearson correlation tests in the SSAP version 11 to identify if there is any significant correlation among the 32 items.

The descriptive data summary is shown in Appendix 3. In Table 1, 12 items with the highest rating are listed. It can be observed that the 12 items that best describe the traits or behaviours of a good PTL are related directly or indirectly to the interaction between the PTL and the students.

Table 1: Ranking of the top 12 items that best describe traits or behaviors of PTL

Ranking By rating	Item	Rating
1	Good presentation skills	4.84
2	Apply updated real life examples in teaching	4.69
3	Good subject related knowledge	4.69
4	Share his/her past experience in studying	4.38
5	Provide prompt reply to e-mail or questions	4.38
6	Give students chance to speak and ask questions in class	4.34

7	Spend additional time after class to help	4.28
8	Make the class interesting	4.28
9	Encourage student to study	4.19
10	Good Language skills	4.19
11	Provide opportunity to communicate	4.19
12	Modify course to suit students	4.03

It can be concluded that most of the PTL preferred by the surveyed exhibit a very strong relationship oriented behaviours. They show high dedication to teaching by showing willingness to make the learning experience more meaningful to the students. Other direct measurements of their academic status like their professional qualifications and their academic qualification, or other more indirect measurement like *career achievement, social status,* and even *research and publication activity* are considered as secondary when students choose their good PTL. As a matter of fact, most of the items that are generally considered to be very important by the university are relative less important to the students. The typical examples are *Use New approach in teaching* (3.72), *Research and Publication* (3.34), and *Apply IT in teaching* (3.25).

In a list prepared by Hawkes (University of Arkansas, 1997) who asked students to suggest good teaching practices, seven points were given (See Appendix 4). A comparison between Hawkes's list and the result of this survey can be found in Table 2.

Table 2: Comparing Hawkes's result and that of the current study

Hawkes's result	Corresponding point in this study and their ranking
"Be clear and organized", and "Stress and repeat main points"	1st: Good presentation skills
"The teacher should relate the material to the real world"	2nd: Apply updated real life examples in teaching
"Make adequate time for office hours"	5th: Provide prompt reply to e-mail or questions, and 7th: Spend additional time after class to help
"The class should be interesting"	8th: Make the class interesting
"Empathize with students"	9th: Encourage students to study

Actually, the only item from Hawkes's list that does not have a counterpart in the current study is "Ask for feedback" which, unfortunately, was not covered in the current survey. It may suggest that the result of this study matches really well with the research findings based on US students.

In a Portuguese study, Rego (2003) studies university teachers' classroom behaviour from the point of view of their students. Rego classifies various behaviours of the teachers into: "participatory behaviour"; "practical orientation"; "conscientiousness"; and "courtesy". He finds that there are strong correlation between the rating of the teachers and orientation in these four behaviours. It should be noted that the elements of his "citizenship behaviours" actually are quite similar to most of the high ranking items in the current study. Again, it tends to indicate the current study shows result that are parallel to that of study based on students from a different country.

Table 3: Comparison of Rego's Citizenship behaviours and the result of this study

Rego's Citizenship behaviours	Corresponding point in this study and their ranking
Participatory behaviours (e.g. promotes student participation in the class; dialogues openly with students)	5th Provide prompt reply to e-mail or questions 6th: Give students chance to speak and ask questions in class 11th: Provide opportunity to communicate with lecturers
Practical orientation (e.g. gives examples that are relevant to the student's life; give practical examples to illustrate the subjects)	2nd: Apply updated real life examples in teaching 12th: Modify course content to suit the need/interest of the students
Conscientiousness (e.g. exposes the subjects in an organized way; is methodical in the presentation of the subject)	1st: Good presentation skills
Courtesy	$7^{th:}$ Spend additional time after class to help 9th: Encourage the students to study

It may be interesting to note that some of the results are quite unexpected. It is generally believed that students can be influenced by traits of the PTL and it is expected that "Good physical appearance" and even "High social status" of the PTL may have strong influence on the impression of students. Yet these two items actually have a very low rating in this survey. Even *Giving easy pass* is rated very low by the students. Suggesting that teachers cannot "buy" the respect of their students by giving them easy passes.

Triangulation

As a way of triangulation, the students were also invited to write down, in the order of importance to them; the three criteria that they think the university should use to select their PTL. The idea is that even if they answered the other part of the questionnaire mechanically, those students who take the initiative to answer these extra questions are probably more serious about this survey and their answers can better reflect their true feelings.

Out of the 21 *Most important selecting criteria* thus listed, the 7 items with the highest frequency of appearance were identified. The ranking of these items are compared with the ranking of the 7 most popular items obtained via calculating the rating of the items in the same 32 questionnaires. (See Table 4)

It can be observed that the five of seven items appear on both lists are the same, indicating that there are high reliability in data obtained via these two methods. The same emphasis on behaviours, but not in traits/qualifications, can still be observed. The only exception of the above statement is in the competence

77

item – Good Presentation Skills. This tends to indicated that the students surveyed are mostly "reproductive learners" (Kember, Jenkins & Ng, 2003:247) who "view good teaching as that which clearly and efficiently presents the body of materials they need to remember for their tests and examinations".

Table 4: Comparison of ranking by rating and by frequency)

	Ranking by rating (from 32 samples)	Rating	Ranking by frequency (from 31 samples)	Frequency
1	Good presentation skills	4.84	Good presentation skills	19
2	Apply updated real life examples in teaching	4.69	Good subject related knowledge	16
3	Good subject related knowledge	4.69	Apply updated real life examples in teaching	14
4	Share his/her past experience in studying	4.38	Many years of working experience (non-teaching)	8
5	Provide prompt reply to e-mail or questions	4.38	High academic qualification	8
6	Give students chance to speak and ask questions in class	4.34	Give students chance to speak and ask questions in class	4
7	Spend additional	4.28	Spend additional	4

time after class to help		time after class to help	

Effect of background of the students

As students of different *year of study* were surveyed, the next factor that should be considered is the possible effects of the background of students on their view of the good PTL. Pearson Correlation test was used to analyse the relationship between the preferred traits and behaviours of the PTL and the *Year of Study* of the students. Using a cut off value of 0.05, it can be determined that the only item that has significant correlation with the *Year of study of the students* is the *academic qualification* of the PTL (Pearson correlation coefficient = 0.351). Students who have more studying experience tend to prefer PTL with higher academic qualification. It shows that the university may not have to push for hiring PhD especially for sub-degree programs.

How possible errors in data collection are handled

Effect of possible mechanical answering

It is possible that some of the students may answer the questions mechanically. That is they take all choice number 5 or choice number 4. In order to estimate the effect of this possible error, the author makes the assumption that students that take the additional time to write additional remarks (the most important selection criteria) are more serious about this questionnaire and thus have lower chance of answering mechanically. It turns out that in all the returned questionnaires, students had took the

79

trouble of written down the selection criteria, suggesting that the effect of mechanical answering is relatively small.

Effect of the sixth choice - "Don't know, not sure, no comment"

In calculating the above rating, the computer counts also choice number zero of the Likert scale (*Don't know, not sure, no comment*) and gives it a weighting of 0. In order to determine if this choice may affect the ranking of the most popular items, the author checks the number of students who choose number zero when they answer the questions. It is found that out of all the answers, students selected choice number six only four times. The effect of this factor in the final rating is generally negligible.

Conclusions and recommendations

The survey shows that good part-time lecturers demonstrated some professional practices even when these practices are not required or not even encouraged by the institution. These behaviours cannot be explained simply by the theory that the lecturers are trying to please the clients.

For the management of the university, it is recommended that they should be more realistic about their policies. They should know that many students, especially part-time students still treasure "telling" based teaching and teachers that can do this effectively are more valuable to students and the university. On the other hand, a good PTL will exhibit good citizenship behavior and that will add value to the university. As such, rather than spending a lot of money in recruiting PTL with high professional qualification or high social status, a good presenter with a good human skills will be a much more cost effective choice.

On the other hand, if the university really believes that high calibre staff with high social and academic status are desirable for various reasons, these high flyers should be well trained in their presentation skills and human skills. As it now stands, there is a dissonance of values between the university and one of its most important stakeholders – the students. The students will keep on demanding what they think are important. If such demands are not met effectively by the university, the university may lose its attractiveness to its students.

For the PTL who are teaching students from different programs, it is recommended that they should recognize that students from different background still demand similar things from their teachers. Students surveyed in this study still focus mostly on the more "didactic or teacher-centred instruction" (Grubb, 1999) and PTL that demonstrate this kind of behaviours will be considered as a good teacher.

Limitations for this study

In this pilot study, only about 100 students from a continuous education institution were surveyed. One logical extension for this study would be to survey students from different departments of the same university to see if they showed the same preference. For example, PTL valued by students from the School of Design might exhibit *Recognize and Rewards* behaviours more. A more interesting extension would be to survey students from universities with different employment terms like salary. The result of such study would tell if the traits and behaviours of the good PTL were universal among PTL who received different extrinsic reward form their jobs. The information thus obtained could be very useful to the management of these universities in designing their recruiting and selection systems.

Acknowledgement

The author would like to thank Professor Eric Hoyle of University of Bristol for his helpful suggestions and comments on the draft of this article.

Bibliography

Beck, C. and Kosnik, C. (2003). Contract staff in Preservice teacher Education. *Teaching Education*. 14:2 August, pp.187-200

Bloomer, K. (1980) The teacher as professional and trade unionist. In Hoyle E. and Magarry J. (Ed.) *World Yearbook of Education 1980: the Professional Development of Teachers*. London: Kogan Page.

Broadfoot, P. and Osborn, M. (1993) *Perceptions of teaching: primary school teachers in England and France*. London and New York: Cassell.

Charfauros, K. and Tierney, W. (1999) Part-time Faculty in colleges and Universities: Trends and Challenges in a turbulent Environment. *Journal of Personnel Evaluation in Education*. 13:2. pp. 141-151

Council on Professional Conduct in Education (1995) *Code for the Education Profession of Hong Kong*. Hong Kong: Government Printer.

Fenwick, T. (2003) Flexibility and Individualisation in Adult education work: the case of Portfolio educators, *Journal of Education and works* Vol. 16, No. 2, June, pp165-183.

Gappa, J. and Leslie, D. (1993) *The invisible faculty – improving the status of part-timers in higher education*. New York: Jossey-Bass.

83

Goodson, I and Hargreaves, A. (2003) Educational changes and the crisis of professionalism in Goodson, I. *Professional knowledge Lives –studies in education and change*. Maidenhead: Open University.

Grubb, W. (1999) *Honoured but invisible – an inside look at teaching in community colleges*. New York: Routledge.

Harvard Graduate School of Education (2003) Strengthening the profession – An interview with Warren Professor and HGSE Dean Ellen Condliffe Lagemann. *HGSE News* Available at http://gseweb.harvard.edu/news/features/lagemann11012003.html. Accessed: 2004/06/08.

Hong Kong Economic Times (2003) 0.5 teacher – two people sharing one teaching job. May 15, ppA24.

Hong Kong Economic Times (2004) Two senior managers of Mid-land Property was invited to lecture in the Hong Kong Polytechnic University (in Chinese). April 23, ppD01.

Hoyle, E. (1974) Professionality, professionalism and control in education, *London Educational Review* 3(2)

Hoyle, E. (1980) Professionalization and deprofessionalization in education. In Hoyle E. and Magarry J. (Ed.) *World Yearbook of Education 1980: the Professional Development of Teachers*. London: Kogan Page.

Hoyle, E & John, P. (1995) *Professional Knowledge and Professional Practices*. London: Cassell.

Jacobs, F. (1998) Using part-time faculty more effectively. In Leslie (Ed.) *The growing use of part-time faculty: Understanding causes and effects.* pp.9-18, San Francisco: Jossey-Bass.

Judge, H (1980) Teaching and professionalization: an essay in ambiguity. In Hoyle E. and Magarry J. (Ed.) *World Yearbook of Education 1980: the Professional Development of Teachers.* London: Kogan Page.

Kember, D. Lee, K. and Li, N. (2001) Cultivating a sense of belonging in part-time students. *International Journal of Lifelong Education.* 20:4, July-Aug, pp.326-341.

Kember, D.; Jemkins, W. & Ng, K. (2003) Adult Students' perceptions of good teaching as a function of their conceptions of learning – Part 1. Influencing the development of self-determination. *Studies in continuing education.* 25:2, Nov. pp239-251.

Kydd, L. (1997) Teacher professionalism and Managerialism. In Kydd L, Crawford, M and Riches, C. (Eds.) *Professional development for educational management,* Buckingham: Open University Press.

Li, N. Leung, D. and Kember, D. (2001) Medium of instruction in Hong Kong universities: the mis-match between espoused theory and theory in use. *Higher Education Policy.* 14(4) pp. 293-312.

Margreaves, A. (1994) *Changing teachers, changing times.* London: Cassell.

Open University of Hong Kong (1999). *Tutor orientation and training*. Hong Kong: Open University of Hong Kong.

Pisani, A. and Stott, N. (1998) An investigation of part-time faculty commitment to developmental advising. *Research in Higher Education*. 39:2. pp.121-142

Pollard, A., Broadfoot, P., Croll, P., Osborn, M., and Abbot, D., 1994. *Changing English Primary Schools? The impact of the Education Reform Act at Key Stage One*. London: Cassell.

Poon, T. (2008) "Hong Kong students' perception of professional behaviours of part-time lecturers in higher education". *Conference paper presented virtually at the International Conference of Education, Research and Innovation 2008, The International Association for Technology, Education and Development (IATED)*, Madrid, Spain, 17-19 November.

Rego, A. (2003) Citizenship behaviours of university teachers – The graduates' point of view. *Active learning in higher education*. 4:1, pp.8-23.

Sing Pao (2003) Baptist University implement visiting lecturer system (in Chinese). Sep 10, p.A12.

Sing Tao (2003) Chinese University has five schemes to meet cut in funding (in Chinese). December 08, p.A08.

Sophos, P. (2003) Part-time faculty in Community Colleges: An overview of the issues. *Community College Journal of Research and Practices.* 27, pp.633-637.

Ta Kung Pao (2003) Contracted teachers become the hope of reducing workload (in Chinese). May 06, p.B09.

The Hong Kong Polytechnic University (2004) *Staff handbook 2004.* Available from: https://www2.polyu.edu.hk/staff/staff_handbook/HB2004/pages/contnets.htm (accessed 2004/09/29)

The University of Hong Kong (2001) Interviews with Outstanding Part-time Teachers. *SpaceNews*, Issue no. 10. Available from: www.hkuspace.edu.hk/space/publications/newsletter/10/08.pdf (accessed 2004/06/24)

The University of Hong Kong (2003) *Guidebook for Part-time teachers.* Available from: http://www.hkuspace.edu.hk/teacher/index.php?action=three (accessed 2004/09/29)

Thorsteinson, T. (2003) Job attitudes of part-time vs. Full-time workers: a meta-analytic review. *Journal of Occupational and Organisational Psychology.* June. 76:2. pp.151-178.

Toutkoushian, R. & Bellas, M. (2003) The effects of part-time employment and gender on faculty earnings and satisfaction: Evidence from the NSOPF: 93. *The Journal of Higher Education.* 74:2, pp.172-196.

University of Arkansas (1997) *TFSC Newsletter*: Relative to Teaching..., March. Available from: http://www.uark.edu/misc/tfscinfo/newsletters/1997/1997-03.html (accessed 2004/09/29)

Appendix 1: Summary of survey data (sorted by rating of match)

	N	Min.	Max.	Mean	Std. Dev.
Good Presentation skills	32	2	5	4.84	.628
Apply updated real life example in teaching	32	3	5	4.69	.535
Good subject related knowledge	32	4	5	4.69	.471
Share his/her past experience in studying	32	3	5	4.38	.609
Provide prompt reply to e-mail or questions	32	3	5	4.38	.793
Give students chance to speak and ask questions	32	4	5	4.34	.483
Spend additional time after class to help	32	3	5	4.28	.683
Make the class interesting	32	3	5	4.28	.772
Encourage students to study	32	3	5	4.19	.693
Good Language skills	32	3	5	4.19	.644
Provide opportunity to communication	32	2	5	4.19	.738
Modify course to suit the needs of the students	32	1	5	4.03	.897
Keep smiling	32	2	5	3.81	.821
Lots of teaching experience	32	2	5	3.81	.738
High professional qualification	32	2	5	3.78	.832
Non teaching working exp.	32	2	5	3.78	.870
Use new teaching approach	32	0	5	3.72	.958
High academic qualification	32	2	5	3.69	.896
Give career consulting	32	2	5	3.66	.902
Recognize good performance	32	2	5	3.44	.914
High career achievement	32	0	5	3.41	1.241
Active in research/publication	32	2	5	3.34	.827
Give tips/hint for exam	32	1	5	3.31	.896
Good computer skills	32	1	5	3.28	.851
Apply IT in teaching	32	2	5	3.25	.718
Speak Cantonese	32	1	5	3.13	.833
Psychological consulting	32	0	5	3.03	1.121
Good physical appearance	32	1	5	2.91	.963
Easy pass	32	1	5	2.91	1.228
High social status	32	0	5	2.69	1.091
Valid N (listwise)	32				

* Items listed in shading are related to traits of the PTL

4   The tail that flips the dog

- Education policies related to the Associate Degree Programmes of Hong Kong

Introduction

Taylor et. al. (1997: 35) describe policy analysis as "the study of what governments do, why and with what effect". In this essay, the government policies related to the Associate Degree (AD) programmes in Hong Kong is discussed under the framework suggested by Vidovich (2002). This essay will focus its attention on the policies that had been promulgated during the period that started roughly from 1999 to 2004 to demonstrate the fact that institutions other than the state government can play a very important role in creation of educational policy. However, as government policies are generally lagging behind the reality, materials from as recent as early 2005 will be used to supplement the discussion. Secondary information collected from academic journals, internet, government documents, and local publications will be the base of this essay.

What is AD

The idea of AD is not originated from Hong Kong. The introduction of this system in Hong Kong fits in well with what Dale (1999) describe as "borrowing" of an idea from mostly the American education system. In The United States and Canada, AD is the degree awarded by community colleges when a student completes a course of study equivalent to the first two years in a four-year college or university. (TheFreeDictionary.com, 2005)

In UK, the Foundation Degree is equivalent to AD. In the mainland of China, although the name "associate degree" is not used, its close equivalent has been offered since 1999. In Taiwan, starting from about the same time, AD has been awarded by officially recognized community colleges (FCE report, 2001). In Australia, two-year associate degree programmes were introduced into Australia in 2004. (TheFreeDictionary.com)

As an academic qualification, AD is the lowest in the hierarchy of academic degrees offered by Canada and the US. The institutions that offered AD programmes are often called community colleges or junior colleges in US. They are usually educational institutions providing post-secondary education and lower-level tertiary education. They often follow an "open admission" policy and students may be admitted even if they do not fit the admission requirements of traditional universities. As these community colleges usually charge a lower tuition than regular universities, students from lower income groups and students not yet academically prepared for a university curriculum are often attracted to them (TheFreeDictionary.com). According to American Association of Community Colleges (2005), 46% of all U.S. undergraduates and 45% of first-time freshmen are studying in community colleges.

AD in Hong Kong

As part of the reform of the overall education system, the government of Hong Kong announced in 2000 an ambitious plan to enlarge the student body of the post-secondary education (Lee and Young, 2003). The Chief Executive of Hong Kong set the target of letting 60% of Hong Kong senior secondary school leavers receive tertiary education within 10 years (HKSAR Chief Executive Policy address, 2000). As a lot of the existing Hong Kong high school leavers are not prepared for the traditional entrance requirements of the regular university programmes (Legislative Council 2001a: 7), and traditional universities are not flexible enough to accept this new influx of students, various new supplementary programmes are needed. In the words of Boshier (2003: 204) "Because schools, universities and tertiary institutions resist change, the most obvious changes will involve adult and continuing education and possible creation of community colleges."

According to the report produced by the Federation of Continuing Education in Tertiary Institutions (FCE), AD programmes were introduced in 2000 by Continuing education (CE) colleges affiliated to universities (FCE Report, 2001) and they have grown very fast. The number of AD student increased from approximately 1000 when the programmes started in 2000 to 10,000 in 2003 (*Ming Pao*, 2004/Dec/02). By the year 2004-5, there are 15 providers in Hong Kong providing 92 various AD programmes to students. In terms of number of graduate, about 6400 students graduated from AD programmes in 2003. In 2004, the number of graduates had jumped to about 9000 but this figure is expected to further increase in 2005 and 2006. (*Ming Pao*, 2005/Mar/18)

Table 1: AD programmes in Hong Kong

Year	00-01	01-02	02-03	03-04	04-05
Provider	3	7	12	15	15
Programme	?	16	46	74	92
Prog./Provider	?	2.3	3.8	4.9	6.1

Source: Employment and Manpower Bureau of HKSAR

Data from Table 1 indicates that the number of programmes has increased drastically over the last few years, yet the number of providers has stabilized around 15. Judging also from the fact that the number of programme offered by each provider has increased continuously, it may be concluded that the industry have become mature and larger providers are trying to take more market share by offering more programmes. For example, enrollment of the Hong Kong Community College (HKCC) of the Hong Kong Polytechnic University (PolyU) has increased 70% in just one year – from 2,100 in 2003-4 to 3,700 in 2004-5 (HKCC, 2005). During the same period, the number of programme they offered has increased from 11 to 13.

Development of education policy related to AD in Hong Kong

Education policy in Hong Kong

The education policy of Hong Kong has been the target of criticisms from various authors. Choi (2003: 638) indicated "… educational policies related to education in Hong Kong were top-down affairs pursuing narrowly utilitarian goals and serving managerialist purposes of monitoring and accountability" Boshier echoed Choi's idea by describing the Hong Kong

Education policy as "Educational policy formation is ad hoc and overly dependent on cherry-picking ideas from other jurisdictions – with Chinese contributions often muted or invisible" (Boshier, 2003: 204)

Policies related to AD

The policy that is discussed in this essay is not a formal government legislation. It is rather a document established by the Education and Manpower Bureau (EMB, 2004c) and is called the "Common Descriptors for Associate Degree". This is more like a formal specification for the AD programmes offered by community colleges in Hong Kong.

When the Education Commission's consultative documents "Education Blueprint for the 21st Century" of 1999 proposed to encourage the establishment of various types of post-secondary college (Education Commission, 1999: 22), local tertiary institutions took the cues and actually ventured to offer AD programmes before any government policy was formulated. Within 5 months after the publication of the consultative document by the Education Commission, the University of Hong Kong, the Hong Kong Baptist University and the Chinese University of Hong Kong had respectively announced their plan to offer AD programmes of their own.

Hence the government had to catch up with the reality and commissioned FCE to draft a policy on how AD should be defined and positioned in the Hong Kong education system. The resulting Consultancy Report formed the basis of the philosophy and pedagogy of the AD programmes in Hong Kong. After adding some ideas from other interest groups like the Hong

Kong Council for Academic Accreditation (HKCAA) and some minor modification, the proposal had become the official position of the government. It is fair to say that the providers of AD programmes, through the effort of FCE, actually established their own industrial standard and create the education policy of AD programmes.

Analysis of the education policies according the Vidovich (2001) framework

The Vidovich (2001) framework is a list of questions separated into three groups according to three different contexts of the policy cycle, namely, "influences"; "text production" and "practice/effects" (See Appendix 1). It does not specifically include questions related to the contexts of "outcomes" and "political strategies" but such consideration is already included when the questions are treated in the micro level of policy practices.

The questions should not be treated as definitive or exhaustive. They should rather be treated just like a menu from which relevant questions can be selected according to the nature of the policy. "They might be seen as an elaboration of the 'why', 'how' and 'what' of policy analysis (Kenway, 1990), which Gale (1999) labels as 'ideology', 'discourse' and 'text' respectively. The 'why now' of policy analysis (Taylor et al., 1997) is also added" (Vidovich, 2001: 12).

Context of Influence: What struggles are occurring to influence the policy?

Global and international influences

In the case of Hong Kong, the most significant impact comes from the 1997 issues and the international immigration caused by such issues. In 1989, the Hong Kong government estimated that a large number of highly educated Hong Kong citizens would leave Hong Kong before 1997. The capacity of the universities in Hong Kong was thus increased drastically to compensate for such a loss. (Wu, 1998) Hence, the number of first-year-first-degree students of the University Grants Committee (UGC) funded programmes was thus increased drastically from about 7000 in 1989 to about 15000 in 1995.

Unfortunately, the Asian Financial crisis of 1998 landed a very heavy blow in the economy of Hong Kong and an economic depression followed. Government needed to cut expenditure in higher education without cutting places in higher education system. Introducing self-financed sub-degree programmes as a substitute for the first two years of the government subsidized conventional university programmes is a reflection of the concerns for cost effectiveness (Yu, 2002).

Prevailing ideological, economic and political conditions

In his 2000 policy speech, Mr. Tung Chee Hwa, the Chief Executive of Hong Kong, set the target of letting 60% of Hong Kong senior secondary school leavers receive post-secondary education within 10 years (HKSAR Chief Executive Policy address, 2000). The objectives set by the government then become

- Widening access to higher education to accommodate as many people as possible (Legislative council Panel on education, 2001b),
- Emphasizing a mixture of Broad-based education plus practical specialism (FEC report 2001:18)
- Enhancing Life-long learning opportunities by offering a more diversified higher education structure (FEC report, 2001:18)

All these point to the need for some new programmes that can accommodate students whose abilities and background may be quite different from the traditional university students. If the traditional degree programmes could not meet the demand of this sharp increase in student population and the government did not promise an increase in funding to expand the traditional university programmes, new self-financing supplementary programmes were needed to accommodate this new influx of students.

On the other hand, there are real commercial needs to train technician grade graduates. Based on the government manpower projections (Legislative Council Panel on Education, 2001a: 4), "... *manpower shortages were anticipated with workers with sub-degree qualifications or at associate professional level*". At the same time, the government needs to find ways to raise the level of technology and knowledge of the graduates from the traditional high schools so they can handle the requirements posted by the advances in technology. From the point of view of improving employment, it may be more feasible to provide more resource to nontraditional CE institutions as they are more geared to those low technology workers whose jobs will be lose in the coming few years (Lee, 2005). Sub-degree programmes, operating in self-financing mode, meet the requirements very nicely.

On the political side, the Hong Kong economic was down and government was under very high political pressure to "do something". Government has very real reason to expand the educational system to keep more young people in the schools instead of the streets (Wu, 2001).

The policy elite and the interests they represent

Many parties had the chance to present their viewpoints in the creation of this policy (Legislative Council Panel on Education, 2001a and 2001b). The Hong Kong Council for Academic Accreditation (HKCAA) is the accreditation body whose interest is in how the programmes should be accredited. The Federation for Continuing Education in Tertiary Institutions (FCE) which members are mostly the CE branches of universities which had offered many AD programmes. The management of universities may see this kind of self-financing programmes as a new source of revenue as government is going to cut funding to universities. On the other hand, there are also employees of the universities who see the AD programmes as an outlet of excessive personnel who are going to be eliminated from the regular university programmes as government cut their funding.

The Hong Kong Association for Lifelong Education (HKALE) represented the interests of smaller providers of CE programmes. Some of its members may also be interested in providing the AD programmes at the later date. The Convocation of the Chinese University of Hong Kong presented the result of a survey of the HKCU alumni. It may be fair to say that it represents the interests of the current degree holders. The UGC is a funding agency of the government but it is supposed to work independently.

Legislative council members like Mr. Szeto Wah and Mr. Cheung Man-Kwong represented the interests of the teachers' union (Hong Kong Professional Teachers' Union) the membership of which consists of teachers from both the high school and universities. There are also other legislative council members who were also present in the meetings; however, their associations with the interests groups were not as obvious as that of the other groups.

The Working Group on the Development of Post-secondary Education of the Education Commission (EC) and the various government officials represented the interests of different administrative branches of the government. They all have the common duties to promote the programmes introduced by the government.

Other interest groups attempting to influence the policy

Other interest parties like high school operators, parents, students and critiques of education policy all try to express their opinions through newspaper or other news media. However, their positions tended to be divided and they could not exert a very big impact. For example, while some students worried about the possibility that the AD programmes might become a back door to the university system and hence hurt the reputation of the university graduates; other students embraced the AD programmes as their second chances to the university.

The most/least powerful interests group

The most powerful interests group should be the members of the FCE. Most of the members of the FCE are CE units from the local universities. They are better organized and they have sufficient resources. One added advantage of this group is that they have been running these AD programmes since 2000-01 and it is well accepted by students.

The Government is also a very influential party as it controls the funding and resources and so it has the 'power' and 'legitimacy' (Mitchell et. al., 1997) to set the rules of the game. HKCAA, the accreditation body also has some influences as they can claim they have moral obligation to guide the quality of the AD programme.

On the other hand, the smaller educational institutions who may become the potential providers in the future have little influence in the process. They are less organized and they lack resources. Also, as they did not operate any AD programmes, they lack the legal status to make any claims.

Over what time period did the context of influence evolves

It is hard to determine over what time period the context of influence evolves as the first three community colleges and their related practices were established way before any paper/publication related specifically to such policy has been established. Officially, the key arguments were presented in the two Legislative Council subcommittee meetings which were held in May and June 2001. (Legislative Council Panel on Education, 2001a and 2001b)

Context of policy text production: What struggles are occurring in the production of the policy text?

Interest (stakeholder) groups that are represented in the production of the policy text and those that are excluded

As stated in section 3.1.3, various groups like large providers, small providers, accreditation body, government education commission, government administration, educators (teachers), government funding body and teacher unions are represented in the production of the policy text. The large providers (FCE), the accreditation body (HKCAA), and the government administration are the most influential groups as their opinions are broadly included in the final documents.

On the other hand, the influences of the students, parents, the users' group and other education institutions which can be the potential providers are less obvious. Some of the concerns for the parents, for example, are the concerns over the tuitions and the financial aids. These may be reflected in the comments of the members of the legislative council (Legislative Council Panel on Education, 2001b: 16). However, these are much weaker voices and are usually marginalized.

Processes used in constructing the policy text

In January 2001, FCE was commissioned by the EMB to undertake a consultancy study on AD programmes in Hong Kong. This study covers the philosophy and pedagogy of the

101

existing programmes in Hong Kong and the development of a common descriptor of AD programmes. "This study has facilitated FCE in reaching consensus on a common descriptor in terms of programme structure, entrance requirements, teachers' qualifications, etc." (FCE report, 2001: 11).

By so doing, the government actually recognized the reality that FCE had already established the industrial norm of operations of the AD programme. It will be very difficult for the government to turn around and ask the FCE members to change what they had done and start a new game. So the government was in fact asking the FCE members to sort out their differences and come up with a system that the government can accept. FCE did come up with such a proposal which after some minor modification, become the base of the framework presented to the Legislative Council Panel on Education for debate. The final policy was not much different from the FCE proposal.

Compromises are made between the different interest (stakeholder) groups

As previously stated, the FCE and the HKCAA are the two most influential stakeholders in the process of creating the document. According to the Power/interest matrix (Scholes, 2001), they are both "key players" that the government have to worry about. However, as the interests of both players were different, conflict can be easily avoided and a compromise could be easily reached. For example, the FCE report was rather specific on how AD programmes offered by accredited institutions (that is, the universities themselves) should be handled, but relatively silent in the accreditation of programmes offered by other institutions. As for the HKCAA, their main concern seems to be that the local accreditation bodies should have the authority to accredit the programmes offered by the non-accredited institutions. The government then had an easy job of combing the suggestions from both reports.

Obviously, it is impossible for the government to follow everything suggested by these "key players". However, compromises were reached in most of the key items except the entry requirement of the students.

Whose interests are the policy intended to serve?

As the policy is packaged as a policy to increase the post-secondary education opportunities, the students are obviously the most direct interest group that the policy should serve. The students have now a more diversified route to their degrees and they get a more broad-based education.

The groups that are indirectly served included the parents and the providers. The parents can be benefited by the financial assistance to the students. As for the providers, they can also apply for the interest free loan and land to start their AD programmes.

Less obviously, the policy also serves the interest of the government. The government can increase its chance of achieving its stated objective of increasing the number of people receiving higher education without more direct financial subsidiary from the government.

The stated intention or purpose of the policy

As stated in the official document (Education and Manpower Bureau, 2004c), the general objectives of the Policy in Expansion in Post-secondary Education Opportunities are:

- "to support the progressive increase in post-secondary education. Our planning target is that by 2010/11, 60% of our senior secondary school leavers will have access to post-secondary education

- to facilitate tertiary institutions, private enterprises and other organizations to provide option(s) other than traditional sixth form education, such as professional diploma courses, and allocate more resources by providing land and loans to those institutions interested in offering such courses

- to extend the scope of assistance offered to students under the Non-means-tested Loan Scheme and low interest loan scheme, and to offer fee remission to the most needy students"

'Hidden' agendas?

As the word 'Hidden' implies, these agendas are not apparent or evident. One possible example can be: The CE branches of the universities want to take a more prominent position in the higher education system. They are "committed" to this idea of expansion in Post-secondary education opportunities as they see this as a chance to "help these once-peripheral divisions lead themselves forward and market their services to the public" (Post, 2003: 992)

On the other hand, the government may have other ideas in its mind when they promote the AD programme. A student in traditional university programme has to pay around HK$40,000 per year and the government has to subsidize, for that student, the university about HK$180,000 per year (*Wen Wei Po*, 2004/Oct/07), whereas a lot of AD programmes which receive no subsidiary from the government charge students below HK$40,000 per year (HKCC, 2005). The whole scheme is a bargain for both the student and the government.

Values reflected in the policy

Diversity, life-long learning and all-round development should be the main values reflected in the policy. (Legislative Council Panel on Education, 2001b: 16)

Intended audience, language and format

The intended audience of the policy is the general public. As the main purpose of the policy is for the public to understand the intention of the government, the language and format it uses is rather simple and easily to understand. The policy has both Chinese and English version so no language barrier is created for the vast majority of the population. It is also posted on the internet where it is easily accessed by the general public.

Steps for 'implementation'

Interesting enough, there is no clear steps for implementation set up in the policy. Part of the reason may be that the AD programmes had been offered by some providers for some time and the policy is just a document to legalize what they had done. Hence, no suitable implementation schedule can be established.

Funding

As the AD is mostly a self-financed programme, the government did not give any direct funding to the providers. The only exception was CityU which converted their UGC funded HD programmes to AD programmes. However, the government later cut their funding to these 'converted' programmes. However, assistance from government is provided in the form of interest-free start-up loans; land grant at nominal premium; accreditation grant and reimbursement of government rents and rates. The total funding is estimated to be about 100 billion Hong Kong dollars (*Ta Kung Pao*, 2001/May/31).

On the other hand, local students pursuing self-financing accredited post-secondary education courses are also supported by Financial Assistance Scheme for Post-secondary Students; non-means-tested Loan Scheme; and Student Travel Subsidy.

Some funding arrangement were not mentioned in the policy itself but they were established to facilitate the implementation of the policy. Government is offering financial support to traditional universities to offer more places in their programmes to facilitate the articulation of AD graduates to the second year and then the third year of their degree programmes. (Wong and Lo, 2005)

Context of practice/effects: What struggles are occurring over the policy practices/effects?

Differences in policy practices between, and within, different localized sites

The policy gives a lot of flexibility in the design of curriculum. Hence, providers tend to offer different programmes according to their expertise and their perception of the market situations. For examples, HKCC offers AD programmes which focus in areas including Business, Design, Engineering, Information Technology and even Beauty and Health Therapy (HKCC, 2005).

In terms of the format of the programme, different providers offered different form of the AD programmes. For example, SPACE of HKU used to offer a three years programme and accept students in both first and second year. However, the current industrial norm is a two years programme that accepts only S7 leavers.

On the other hand, there were criticisms that some providers who do not follow the minimum entry requirement and are accepting S6 leavers under certain special conditions. Other than periodically sending out memo containing the common descriptors for associate degree, EMB so far has not been very active in reinforcing the minimum entry requirement.

Global/international influences evident in the policy practices at local levels

The influences are mostly in the form of articulations. To increase the popularity of their AD programmes, providers set up various top-up programmes for their AD graduates. Most of the providers set up joint ventures with overseas universities to offer top up programmes that will accept AD graduates. Providers which fail to offer such top up programmes face a very big competitive disadvantage.

On the other hand, some providers also try to promote their AD programmes in teaching center located outside Hong Kong. So far, most of these "overseas" programmes are located in the mainland of PRC (*HKET*, 2004/Aug/06). In the future, however, there is nothing to stop these providers to offer their programmes in other countries.

How open is the policy to interpretation by practitioners?

The text of the policy is not very complicated and is generally quite simple to understand. The main issue is not in the document itself, but in the fact that the providers are pushing for expansion of the programmes. The providers are interested in extending this programme that is originally designed mostly for the local students to cover students from other regions (mostly the mainland) and countries (*Sing Pao Daily News*, 2004/Feb/11).

How well is the policy received?

Initially, the AD programme was rejected by a lot of people as being unrealistic. Educators and politicians worried that the AD graduates would not be able to articulate to the regular universities programmes and AD would become a 'path with no exit' (*Ming Pao*, 2001/May/16)

Other critiques focus on the fact the AD programmes may become a 'second chance' for the students who are not qualified to enter universities via the traditional ways. If these graduates of these AD programmes are later accepted into the university programmes, they would lower the overall academic level of the Hong Kong universities. (*Ta Kung Pao*, 2001/Jul/29)

A more recent survey found that 53% of the parents supported their children to join the AD or HD programmes but they find it unreasonable that the government does not provide more financial support to the AD students. (*Sun Daily*, 2005/Jan/17)

Another more encouraging report showed that about 74% of the AD graduates from HKCC can continuous their education in other institutions (HKCC, 2005). When more and more AD graduates successfully find a place in other university programmes or in the job market, the acceptance of the AD programmes will increase.

To what extent is the policy (actively or passively) resisted?

Educators not in the CE area were worried about the legal status of the AD. They were also worried about the progression pathways of AD programmes as no university in Hong Kong had made such commitment of accepting AD graduates to their degree programmes. Even if they were willing to do that, there would not be enough places in their year two programmes to accommodate these AD graduates (Legislative Council Panel on Education, 2001a:8-9). However, these resistances were pretty much individualized. There was not much resistance from the universities as the majority of the providers were the CE branches of these universities. They had offered the AD programmes since 2000 and the market acceptance had been quite encouraging.

To what extent is the policy transformed within individual institutions?

For the successful providers like HKCC, the major transform is in the expansion of the programmes in terms of enrolments; number of programme offered; mode of offering; and geographical scope of operation. As competition grows, there may also be new focuses in areas that are not emphasized by the original policy. For example, social activities, campus life had become the selling points of HKCC's AD programmes. (HKCC, 2005)

Are practitioners at the local level empowered by the policy?

The policy gives the providers the legal right to do what they had been doing. The providers from large universities officially acquired self-accreditation status. Other approved accreditation bodies are also empowered to accredit the AD programmes from smaller or newer providers.

Response to localized needs

Providers are more responsive to the market needs than the policy and they move quickly to meet the market demand. For examples, providers are very quick in offering new programmes in any subject area that showed an increase in demand. Also, efforts had been spent in attracting AD students from the mainland. As a first step, various providers are going to establish branches in mainland China. (*Wen Wei Po*, 2004/Oct/07). The main attraction to the students is that the graduates from these AD programmes can then join directly the third year of the overseas universities. (*Ta Kung Pao*, 2004/Oct/07)

Unintended consequences

EMB is considering the proposal of allowing students from mainland China to join the Hong Kong AD programmes in 2005 or 2006. This is going to open up a big market for the providers of the AD programme (*HKET*, 2004/Aug/06). The Federation of Higher Education is contemplating requesting the government to allow these AD graduates from mainland to complete their study for bachelor degree in Hong Kong. According to the current immigration practices, students who have completed their bachelor degree in Hong Kong will then be allowed to stay and take up employment in Hong Kong. (*Sing Pao Daily News*, 2004/Feb/11) As such, the AD programmes can be a very attractive route for those who seek a residence in Hong Kong. Unfortunately, governments from both Hong Kong and mainland had not come up with the proper rules and regulations specifying how this should be done. (*Sing Pao Daily News*, 2004/Jul/31)

Hence the stakeholders of a policy involve not just one government and the people under its jurisdiction. It may even require cooperation and support from the government of two different places. This external effect on policy is not listed in Dale's typology of mechanism of external effects on national policies (Dale, 1999).

Winners and losers

One obvious winner will be the groups of students who do not meet the requirements to enter universities via the traditional routes. They now get a second chance. It is true that the new policy remove the hope that the government will subsidize their courses and they will have to come up with the financial resources to pay the tuition but at least they get a chance to access higher education.

In the long run, most of the university operators will be benefited. In a few years, when the number of AD graduates reaches 20,000 per years but the places offered in traditional university programmes increase by only a few thousands, there will a very high demand for top-up degree programmes offered by both local and overseas universities.

Less obviously, the group that are most benefited by this policy is the CE unites of the big universities like the SPACE of The University of Hong Kong, and the HKCC of the Hong Kong Polytechnic University. CE units of large universities get a chance to move to the front and expand very quickly by offering both AD and top up programmes. On the other hand, the government has offered interest free loans and nine plots of land for the providers to build campus for their community colleges. Theoretically, providers could all bid for these resources. However, 85% of the loan and four of the nine plots were finally rewarded to the seven traditional universities and their affiliated institutions. Smaller providers were either not awarded the land or they are not rewarded the loan because they do not have sufficient financial supports to meet the requirements of the government. (*Sing Tao Daily*, 2005 Mar 09). The net result is that the policy is in favour of the larger institutions.

One of the obvious losers of this policy can be the high schools in Hong Kong. S7 students who have failed to achieve an average grades in the Hong Kong Advanced Level Examination (HKALE) have not much chance to enter universities, many of them repeat their S7 year, hoping that they will eventually improve their grades. Many of these students can now opt for the AD programmes and will eventually get their degree via articulating back to the traditional degree programmes or the top up degree programmes. Similarly, S5 leavers who failed the Hong Kong Certificate of Education Examination (HKCEE) can now choose the Pre-AD programmes. In either case, traditional high schools will loss students and revenues.

Similarly, as more and more paths for higher education are now available locally, fewer students are going to study overseas (HKET, 2004/Oct/13). Overseas educational providers in Hong Kong will lose part of their potential market (Legislative Council Panel on Education, 2001b: 7)

In 2004, the FCE proposed that the government should relax the entrance requirements of the AD programme. Instead of F.7 graduates, F.6 graduates with better result in school certificate examination shall be allowed to enter the AD programme provided that they also pass an interview (Young, 2004). This is going to increase the loss of the high school operators.

Conclusion

According to the projection of the government, there could be a possible excess of 230,000 workers with relative low educational attainment by 2007. "In anticipation of changes in the job market, we vigorously encourage both job seekers and employees to upgrade themselves by learning". (HKSAR Chief Executive Policy Address, 2005:13). Hence, the growth of the AD programmes is expected to continuous.

It can be conclude that the creation of the policy related to the AD programmes exemplified a new way of policy making. In many occasions, the practitioners take the more proactive role and the government is actually led by the practitioners and different interest groups. In Boshier's (2003:204) words, "In the past, educational policy was pronounced from on high. But now an increasingly well-educated and informed citizenry is shaking–up the policy process".

Acknowledgement

The author would like to thank Professor Susan Robertson of University of Bristol for her suggestions and comments on the draft of this article.

Bibliography

Apple Daily (2004) 'Last year population was 6.81 million; just increase 0.35%, lowest increase since returning to China' (in Chinese). February 18, p.A12.

American Association of Community Colleges, Available at: http://www/aacc/nche.edu. Accessed: 2005/Mar/21.

Boshier, R. (2003) Review of *Lifelong Learning in Action: Hong Kong Practitioners' Perspectives* by Gribbin, J. and Kennedy, P. (eds.) *International Journal of Lifelong Education*, 22(2), pp203-05.

Bray M. (1997) 'Education and Colonial Transition: the Hong Kong experience in comparative perspective'. In Bray M. and Lee W. (eds.) *Education and Political transition: implications of Hong Kong's change of sovereignty*. Hong Kong: Comparative Education Research Centre.

Chan, M. (2002) Introduction: The Hong Kong SAR in Flux. In Chan, M and So A. (eds.), *Crisis and Transformation in China's Hong Kong*. Armonk: Sharp.

Chau G. and Chan T. (2001) 'Challenges faced by accountancy education during and beyond the years of transition – some Hong Kong evidence'. *Journal of Accounting Education*. 19(3) Autumn, pp.145-162.

Cheng, J. (1995) *Hong Kong education during political transformation*. (In Chinese) Hong Kong: Oxford University Press.

Choi, P. (2003) "Introduction: Education policy in Hong Kong', Journal of Education Policy, 18(6) pp.637-9.

Cummings. T. and Worley, C. (2001) *Organisational Development and Change*, 6th ed. Cincinnati: South-Western

Dale, R. (1999) Specifying globalisation effects on national policy: a focus on the mechanisms, *J. of Education Policy*, 14(1), pp. 1-17.

Education and Manpower Bureau (2004c), 'Policy Highlights: Expansion in Post- secondary Education Opportunities', available   in:
http://www.emb.gov.hk/index.aspx?langno=1&nodeid=1355#pr ogrammes
Accessed: 2005/Mar/25

Education and Manpower Bureau (2004d), 'Common Descriptors on Associate Degree: Programme Objectives', available   in:
http://www.emb.gov.hk/index.aspx?nodeID=1211&langno=1
Accessed: 2005/May/14

Evans, T. and Tregenza, K. (2002) 'Asian students' experience of studying overseas courses'. In Murphy, D.; Shin, N. and Zhang, W. (Eds.) *Advancing Online Learning in Asia*. Hong Kong: Open University of Hong Kong Press.

Federation for continuing education in Tertiary Institutions (2001) *The Associate Degree in Hong Kong - Final report of a Consultancy Study commissioned by the Education and*

*Manpower Bureau and undertaken by the Federation for Continuing Education in Tertiary Institutions. A*vailable in: http://www.fce.org.hk/~fceorg/ADInHK.pdf   Accessed: 2004/Nov/24.

Hang Seng Bank Limited (2004) 'Employment challenges'. *Hang Seng Economic Monthly*. March.

HKSAR Chief Executive's Policy address 2000, (2000) Available at: http://www.policyaddress.gov.hk/pa00/p66e.htm, Accessed: 17 July, 2004.

HKSAR Chief Executive's Policy address 2005 (2005) Available   at: http://www.policyaddress.gov.hk/2005/eng/pdf/speech.pdf, Accessed: 14, March, 2005.

Hong Kong Census & Statistic Department (2004) Population and   Vital   Events.   Available   at http://www.info.gov.hk/censtatd/eng/hkstat/hkinf/population_in dex.html, Accessed: 2004/May/17

Hong Kong Commercial Daily (2004) 'Arthur Li: It is natural for Hong Kong people to be pro China' (in Chinese). April 20, p.A05.

Hong Kong Community College (2005), *2005 Guide to Associate Degree programmes*. Hong Kong: Hong Kong Community College.

Hong Kong Economic Times (2004a) 'Five universities perform well in division of labour – total bonus of 25 million dollars was rewarded' (in Chinese). March 25. p.A34

Hong Kong Economic Times (2004b) 'City University struggles to attract students form the mainland', hoping to increase to 150 students (in Chinese) April 21. p.A23

Hong Kong Economic Times (2004c) 'Beijing and Qing Hua University accept students without examination' (in Chinese). June 07, p.A22.

Hong Kong Economic Times (2004d) 'SPACE plans to open branch in Su Zhou for AD programmes' (in Chinese). Aug 06, p.A28.

Hong Kong Economic Times (2004e) 'Less students are studying in overseas due to competition from AD programmes' (in Chinese). Oct 13, p.A30.

Hong Kong Education and Manpower Bureau (2004a) Statistical Information. Available at http://www.emb.gov.hk/index.aspx?nodeID=75&langno=1. Accessed: 2004/April/18.

Hong Kong Education and Manpower Bureau (2004b) Memorandum of Understanding between the Mainland and Hong Kong on Mutual Recognition of Academic Degrees in Higher Education. Available at http://www.emb.gov.hk/index.aspx?nodeID=2491&langno=2 Accessed: 2004/April/18.

Hong Kong iMail (2002) 'Academics join in call for Arthur Li apology'. October 24.

Hong Kong Polytechnic University (2004a) 'New Human resource model approved'. *Staff newsletter of The Hong Kong Polytechnic University*. March/April 2004. Available at http://www2.polyu.edu.hk/script/staff/ePost@PolyU. Accessed: 2004/March 04.

Hong Kong Polytechnic University (2004b) 'Role of PolyU re-affirmed'. *Staff newsletter of The Hong Kong Polytechnic University*. March/April 2004. Available at http://www2.polyu.edu.hk/script/staff/ePost@PolyU. Accessed: 2004/March 04.

Jegede, O. (2001) 'Hong Kong'. In Jegede, O. and Shive, G. (eds.) *Open and distance education in the Asia Pacific Region*, p.44. Hong Kong: Open University of Hong Kong Press.

Ku, A. (2002) 'Postcolonial cultural Trends in Hong Kong: Imaging the Local, the National, and the Global'. In Chan, M and So, A. (Eds.), *Crisis and Transformation in China's Hong Kong*. Armonk: Sharp

Law, W. (1997) 'The accommodation and resistance to the decolonisation, neocolonisation and recolonisation of higher education in Hong Kong'. *Comparative Education*. 33:2, pp.187-209.

Lee H. (2005) 'The basic cure for the problems is in improving the quality of labours' (in Chinese) Hong Kong Financial Journal, Jan 17, p.P24.

Legislative Council Panel on Education (2001a), subcommittee on increase in post-secondary education opportunities. Minutes of meeting held on Tuesday, 15 May 2001, LC Paper No. CB(2)2385/00-01.

Legislative Council Panel on Education (2001b), subcommittee on increase in post-secondary education opportunities. Minutes of meeting held on Friday, 1 June 2001. LC Paper No. CB(2)185/01-02.

Lei, J. (2003) 'This is not the way to manage university education'. (In Chinese). *Ming Pao*. November 19, p.D8.

Lui, F. (2002) 'Hong Kong's Economy since 1997'. In Chan, M and So A. (eds.), *Crisis and Transformation in China's Hong Kong*. Armonk: Sharp

Luk, B. (2003) 'Chinese culture in the Hong Kong curriculum: heritage and colonialism'. In Stimpson, P.; Morris, P.; Fung, Y. and Carr, R. (Eds.), *Curriculum, Learning and Assessment: the Hong Kong experience.* Hong Kong: Open University of Hong Kong Press.

Ming Pao, (2001) 'Setting a target that 60% of students can study in higher education is unrealistic' (in Chinese), May 16, p.B16.

Ming Pao, (2003) 'City U Associate programmes plan for 35% salary reduction, increase teacher to student ratio and new staff will be hired only under contract system'. (in Chinese). October 03,. p.A16.

Ming Pao, (2004a) 'Polytechnic University resumes renewing long term employment contracts with staff' (in Chinese), April 14, p.A02.

Ming Pao, (2004b) 'Members of the Federation of continuous education has united goals' (in Chinese), Dec 02, p.E01.

Ming Pao, (2005) 'SPEED top up programmes train talent for various industries' (in Chinese), Mar 18, p.A37.

Mitchell, R., Agle, B. and Wood, D. (1997) 'Toward a theory of stakeholder identification and salience: defining the principle of who and what really counts', *Academy of Management Review*, 22(4), pp853-66.

Mok, K (1999) 'The cost of managerialism: The implications for the "McDonaldisation" of higher education in Hong Kong'. *Journal of Higher Education Policy and Management*. May, 21, pp.117-127.

Mok, K and Lee, H (2000) 'Globalization or re-colonization: higher education reforms in Hong Kong'. *Higher Education Policy*. 13, pp.361-377.

Ni, Q. (2004) 'American educational exhibition attracts thousands' (in Chinese). *Apple Daily*. April 4, p.A10.

Ng, T. (2004a) 'Universities set performance targets'. *The Hong Kong Standard*. January 31. p.B06.

Ng, T. (2004b) 'Colleges to target overseas students'. *The Hong Kong Standard.* April 21, p.B03.

Oriental Daily (2004a) 'Hong Kong universities will be able to recruit students from the mainland' (in Chinese). April 8, p.A24.

Oriental Daily (2004b) 'Low birth rate causes 22 kindergartens to close down' (in Chinese). April 8. p.A24

Oriental Daily (2004c) 'Education reform has strong impact on AL Colleges' (in Chinese), Oct. 22, p.A28.

Oriental Daily (2005) 'Bachelor Degrees from so and so college' (in Chinese). Jan 15. p.B12.

Poon, C. (2003) Script delivered in RTHK radio programme "Letter to Hong Kong" on 1 November 2003.

Post, D. (2003) 'Post-secondary education in Hong Kong – Repercussion for inequality and civil society'. *Asian Survey.* 43:6, pp.989-1011.

Postiglione, G. (2002) 'The transformation of Academic Autonomy in Hong Kong'. In Chan, M and So A. (eds.), *Crisis and Transformation in China's Hong Kong.* Armonk: Sharp

Scholes, K. (2001) 'Stakeholder mapping: a practical tool for public sector managers' in Johnson, G. and Scholes, K. (eds), *Exploring Public Sector Strategy*, Financial Times/Prentice Hall.

Shive, G. (1992) 'Educational Expansion and the Labor Force', in Postiglione, G. and Leung, J. (eds.) *Education and society in*

Hong Kong: Toward one country and two systems. pp.215-231. Hong Kong: Hong Kong University Press.

Sing Pao Daily News (2004) "Institution planned to recruit AD students from mainland in September' (in Chinese). Feb. 11, p.A03.

Sing Tao Daily, (2004) 'Land for community colleges are awarded mostly to universities' (in Chinese), Mar, 09, p.F01.

Slaughter, S. and Leslie, L. (1997) *Academic capitalism – Politics, policies, and the entrepreneurial university*. Baltimore: The Jones-Hopkins University Press.

So, A and Chan, M. (2002) 'Conclusion: Crisis and transformation in the Hong Kong SAR – Toward Soft authoritarian Developmentalism?' In Chan, M and So A. (eds.) *Crisis and Transformation in China's Hong Kong*. Armonk: Sharp

Sun Daily (2005) 'Unreasonable for AD graduates to get a lower salary' (in Chinese), Jan 17, p.A30.

Sutherland, S. (2002), '*Higher Education in Hong Kong - Report of the University Grants Committee commissioned by the Secretary for Education and Manpower*', Available at: http://www.ugc.edu.hk/english/documents/UGCpubs/her_e.html. Accessed: 10 December 2003.

Ta Kung Pao, (2001) 'Places for AD programmes will increase by 20,000 in 10 years' (in Chinese), May 31, p.B06.

Ta Kung Pao, (2001) 'Associate Degree' (in Chinese), Jul 29, p.C03.

Ta Kung Pao, (2004) 'HKU Space recruits AD students in Su Zhou' (in Chinese), Oct 19, p.A17.

Taylor, S., Rizvi, F., Lingard, B., and Henry, M. (1997) *Educational Policy and the Politics of Change*, London: Routledge.

TheFreeDictionary.com, available at: http://encyclopedia.thefreedictionary.com/associate's%20degree. Accessed: 2005/Mar/21.

Thomas, R. (1983) 'The two colonies – A prologue'. In Thomas, R. and Postlethwaite N. (eds.) *Schooling in East Asia – Forces of change*. Oxford: Pergamon Press.

Thomas, R. and Postlethwaite N. (1983) 'Describing change and estimating its causes'. In Thomas, R. and Postlethwaite N. (eds.) *Schooling in East Asia – Forces of change*. Oxford: Pergamon Press.

Thompson, A. and Strickland, A. (2001) *Crafting and Executing Strategy – Text and Readings*. Boston: McGraw Hill.

University Grants Committee, (2002a), *Higher Education Review*, [Online] Available at: [http://www.ugc.edu.hk/english/documents/press/her2603e.html], (Accessed: 22 December 2003)

University Grants Committee, (2002b), *UGC's Final Recommendations,* Available at: http://www.ugc.edu.hk/english/documents/press/pr271102e.html. Accessed: 10 December 2003.

University Grants Committee, (2003a) '2nd TLQPR of Hong Kong Baptist University (Sept 2003)', Available at: http://www.hkbu.edu.hk/2nd_tlqpr/. Accessed: 18 December 2003.

Wen Wei Po (2004) 'HKU SPACE will establish a branch in Su Zhou' (in Chinese), Oct 07, p.A23.

Wong, K. and Lo, Y. (2005) 'HK$6 trillion to increase places in universities to help AD graduates' (in Chinese), *Wen Wai Po.* Jan 13, p.Z08.

Wu S. (2001), 'Prosperity in U.S. does not guarantee prosperity in Hong Kong', (in Chinese), *Apple Daily*, Oct 06, p.B02.

Young C. (2004) 'F.6 graduates may enter AD programme' (in Chinese), *Sing Tao Daily*, Oct 21, p.A04.

Yu J. (2002) 'The great laps forward of the AD programme' (in Chinese), *Hong Kong Economic Journal*, Jun 13, p.P08.

Zheng, C. (2003). 'The causes of funding cut of the universities' (in Chinese). *Hong Kong Economic Journal*, November, 19, p.9.

Appendix 1: The original Vidovich (2002) framework

Context of Influence: What struggles are occurring to influence the policy?

- Are global influence and trends evident in this policy domain?
- Are there international influences being brought to bear? If so which are the key nation-states involved?
- How are global and international influences operating?
- To what extent are global and international level influences mediated within the nation-state?
- Who are the policy elite and what interests do they represent?
- Which other interest groups are attempting to influence policy?
- Which interests are most/least powerful and why?
- Over what time period did the context of influence evolve before they policy was constructed?

Context of policy text production: What struggles are occurring in the production of the policy text?

- Which interest (stakeholder) groups are represented in the production of the policy text and which are excluded?
- What processes are used to construct the policy text and why?
- What compromises are made between the different interest (stakeholder) groups and how were they achieved?
- Whose interests are the policy intended to serve?
- What are the dominant discourses of the policy text and which discourses are excluded?
- What is the stated intention or purpose of the policy?
- Are there any 'hidden' agendas?

- Which values are reflected in the policy?
- What are the issues that constitute the focus of the policy, and do they relate to global/international policy agendas?
- What are the key concepts of the policy?
- What is the format of the policy and why?
- What is the language of the policy and why?
- Are there inconsistencies and contradictions in the policy texts?
- Who is the intended audience of the policy text?
- How accessible or understandable is the policy text to the audience?
- Are the steps for 'implementation' set out as part of the policy text?
- Is the 'implementation' funded?
- Is there a specified mechanism to evaluate the policy?

Context of practice/effects: What struggles are occurring over the policy practices/effects?
- Is this policy being practiced in a wide variety of localised contexts?
- How different are the policy practices between, and within, different localized sites?
- Are global/international influences evident in the policy practices at local levels?
- Who can access the policy and who does access it?
- How open is the policy to interpretation by practitioners?
- How well is the policy received?
- Who put the policy into practice?
- What processes are used to put the policy into practice and why?
- To what extent is the policy (actively or passively) resisted?

127

- Is resistance collective or individual?
- To what extent is the policy transformed within individual institutions?
- How predictable were the policy practices/effects?
- Are practitioners at the local level empowered by the policy?
- Are practitioners at the local level able to respond rapidly to meet localized needs in this policy domain?
- What are the unintended consequences?
- What is the impact of the policy on different localized groupings based on class, gender, ethnicity, rurality and disability?
- Are there winners and losers?